SAMSUNG GALAXY

A53 5G USER GUIDE

THE COMPLETE, COMPREHENSIVE MANUAL TO HELP BEGINNERS AND SENIORS MASTER THE NEW 2022 GALAXY A53 5G LIKE A PRO

GW00457335

BENJAMIN ISRAEL

Contents

INTRODUCTION

The Galaxy A53 5G is a wonderful piece of device released by the tech giant, Samsung.

Over the years, the company has continued to impress its fans with quality products with cutting-edge technology in the world of smartphones.

This device comes with enhanced features from its older sibling, the Galaxy A52.

But having a new device with outstanding features and exceptional functionalities isn't all you need.

You also need to know how to use these features of your device to carry out every day's task – that's when you know the real worth of your device.

This book, therefore, provides you a comprehensive step-by-step guide to mastering all the basic and advanced features, settings and functions, care and maintenance tips, troubleshooting tips, plus a robust index to help you find specific subjects.

CHAPTER 1: BASIC OPERATIONS

Device layout and functions

Speaker — Microphone

Light sensor —

Front camera

Volume key

Touchscreen —

Side key

Fingerprint recognition sensor

SIM card / Memory card tray

Earphone jack / Multipurpose jack (USB Type-C)

GPS antenna

Rear camera

NFC antenna

Flash

Main antenna

Speaker

Microphone

CAUTION:

- When using the speakers, such as when playing media files or using speakerphone, do not put the device near your ears.

- Take care not to expose the camera lens to a strong light source, such as direct sunlight as this may damage the camera image sensor. A damaged image sensor cannot be repaired and will produce dots or spots in pictures.

- If the device's glass or acrylic body is broken, take the device to a Samsung Service Centre for repairs before using it to avoid the risk of injury.

- If dust or foreign materials enter the microphone, speaker, or receiver, the device's sound may be impaired or certain features may not work. Attempting to remove the dust or foreign materials with a sharp object may cause damage to the device and affect its appearance.

NOTE:

- Connectivity problems and battery drain may ensue in the following circumstances:

  - Attaching metallic stickers on the antenna area of the device

  - Attaching a device cover made with metallic material to the device

  - Shielding the device's antenna area with your hands or other objects as you're using certain features, such as calls or the mobile data connection

- It is advisable to use a Samsung-endorsed screen protector. The use of unapproved screen protectors may cause malfunctioning of the sensors.

- Never cover the light sensor area with screen accessories, such as a screen protector, stickers, or a cover as doing so may cause the sensor to malfunction.

Hard keys

Key	Function
Side key	• When the device is off, press and hold to turn it on. • Press to turn on or lock the screen. • Press down to start a conversation with Bixby. See *Using Bixby* for more information. • Double press or press and hold to start any app or feature you set.
Side key + Volume Down key	• Press both keys together at the same time to take a screenshot. • Press and hold at the same time to turn off the device.

Setting the Side key

Choose an app or feature to launch by pressing the Side key twice or pressing and holding the Side key.

Start the **Settings** app, tap **Advanced features** → **Side key**, and then select an option you want.

Soft buttons

Recents button — Back button

Home button

Anytime you turn on the screen, the soft buttons will appear at the bottom of the screen. See *Navigation bar* (soft buttons) for more information.

Charging the battery

Charge the battery before using it for the first time or when it has been unused for prolonged periods.

Wired charging

Connect the device's USB cable to the USB power adaptor and plug the cable into the device's multipurpose jack to charge the battery. After the device is fully charged, disconnect the charger from the device.

Quick charging

From the **Settings** app, tap **Battery and device care** →
Battery → **More battery settings**, and then activate the
feature you want.

- **Fast charging**: To use the fast charging feature, ensure
  you use a battery charger that supports Adaptive fast
  charging.

NOTE: The battery will charge more quickly if the device or
its screen is turned off.

How to charge other devices

Charge another mobile device with your device's battery using the USB cable.

Connect your device and the other device using the USB
cord that came with your device. Depending on the other
device, a USB connection may be required.

When charging begins, the battery charging icon appears on the screen of the other device.

The data transfer pop-up window that displays on your smartphone is for app selection. Selecting an app from the pop-up window is not advised.

Reducing the battery consumption

Your device offers various options that help you conserve battery power.

- Enhance the device using the device care feature.
- When the device is not being used, turn off the screen by pressing the Side key.
- Activate power saving mode.
- Close unnecessary apps.
- Deactivate the Bluetooth feature when you're not using it.
- Deactivate auto-syncing of apps which require syncing.
- Reduce the backlight time.
- Reduce the screen brightness.

Battery charging tips and precautions

- If the battery is totally discharged, the device cannot be turned on instantly when the charger is connected. Allow an empty battery to charge for a few minutes before you turn on the device.

- If you use multiple apps at once, network apps, or apps that need a connection to another device, the battery will empty quickly. To avoid losing power during a data transfer, always use these apps after you've fully charged the battery.

- The charging speed of your device may reduce when you're charging it with other sources of power, e.g. a computer due to a lower electric current.

- The device can be used while charging, but it the battery may take longer time to get fully charged.

- If the device receives an unsteady power supply while charging, the touchscreen may not work. In that case, disconnect the charger from the device.

- While charging, the device and the charger may become hot. This is normal and does not affect the device's lifespan or performance. However, if the battery gets hotter than normal, the charger may stop charging.

- If the multipurpose jack is wet and you use it to charge, it may cause damage to the device.

  Always ensure the multipurpose jack is dry before charging the device.

- If the device is not charging appropriately, take the device and its charger to a Samsung Service Centre.

SIM or USIM card (nano-SIM card)

Insert the SIM or USIM card that you got from by the mobile telephone service provider.

For dual SIM models, you can insert two SIM or USIM cards and you'll have two phone numbers or service providers in one device. In some areas, data transfer speeds may decrease when two SIM cards are inserted in the device than when one SIM card is inserted.

NOTE: Some services requiring a network connection may be unavailable depending on the service provider.

Installing the SIM or USIM card

Single SIM card tray

Dual SIM card tray

<Underside>

1   Push the ejection pin into the hole next to the tray to bring out the tray.

2   Gently pull out the tray from the tray slot.

3   Put the SIM or USIM card on the tray with the gold-col-oured contacts facing downwards and gently press the SIM or USIM card into the tray to make it firm.

4   Carefully insert the tray back into the tray slot.

CAUTION:

•   Press the ejection pin into the **tray's hole** to expose the tray.

•   Use only a nano-SIM card.

•   Be cautious not to lose your SIM or USIM card, or allow others have unauthorized access to it. Samsung does not accept any legal responsibility for any damages or inconveniences experience as a result of lost or stolen cards.

- Check to ascertain hat the ejection pin is perpendicular to the hole. Or else, the device may be damaged.

- If you do not fix the SIM card firmly into the tray, it may fall out of the tray unawares.

- If you insert a wet tray into your device, your device may get damaged. Always make sure the tray is dry before inserting it into your device.

- Ensure the tray is completely inserted into the tray slot to prevent liquid from entering your device.

Correct card installation (dual SIM card tray)

SIM card manager (dual SIM models)

Go to the **Settings** app and launch, then tap **Connections** → **SIM card manager**.

- **SIM cards**: Activate the SIM card to start using it and customize the SIM card settings.

- **Preferred SIM card**: Choose which specific SIM cards you would want to use for some features, such as voice calls, when two cards are activated.

- **Auto data switching:** If the device's primary SIM card can't connect to the network, set it to use another SIM card for data services.

- **More SIM card settings**: Change and personalize the call settings.

Memory card (microSD card)

Installing a memory card

The maximum capacity of memory card you device can hold may differ from other models. Some memory cards may have incompatibility issues with your smartphone. It depends on the manufacturer and type of the memory card. To know your device's maximum memory card capacity, please visit the Samsung website.

1 Safely insert the ejection pin into the hole next to the tray to release the tray.

2 Pull out the tray from the tray slot with caution.

3 Put a memory card on the tray with the gold-coloured contacts facing downwards and gently press the memory card into the tray to make it firm.

4 Insert the tray back into the tray slot carefully.

CAUTION:

• Press the ejection pin into the **tray's hole** to expose the tray.

• Some memory cards may not be wholly compatible with the device. Using a memory card that is not compatible with your device result in damage to the device or the memory card, or corrupt the data you have stored in them.

• Carefully insert the memory card right-side up.

14

- Confirm that the ejection pin is perpendicular to the hole. Or else, the device may get damaged.

- Removing the tray from the device disables the mobile data connection.

- If you don't fix the card firmly into the tray, the memory card may leave or fall out of the tray.

- If you insert a wet tray into your device, the device may be damaged. Always make sure the tray is dry before insert it into your device.

- Be cautious to insert the tray completely into the tray slot to avoid liquid from entering your device.

NOTE:

- The device complies with the FAT and the exFAT file systems for memory cards. When you insert a memory card that has been formatted in a different file system into your device, it will request you to format the card again in your device or else, it will not identify the card. To use the memory card, you must first of all format it. If your device cannot format or identify the memory card, contact the memory card manufacturer or a Samsung Service Centre.

- Frequent writing and erasing of data reduce the lifespan of memory cards.

- When inserting a memory card into the device, you'll see the memory card's file directory in the **My Files** → **SD card** folder.

Removing the memory card

Before removing the memory card, first of all unmount it for safe removal.

From the **Settings** app, tap **Battery and device care** → **Storage**. Take a leftward swipe to view the **SD card** page. Then tap ⋮ and tap **Unmount**.

CAUTION: Never remove external storage, such as a memory card or USB storage, while the device is transferring or accessing information, or right after transferring data. Doing so may lead to data corruption or loss or cause damage to the external storage or device. Samsung does not take responsibility for losses, including loss of data, resulting from the misuse of external storage devices.

Formatting the memory card

A memory card that has been formatted on a computer may not be compatible with the device. It is recommended that you format the memory card on the device.

Launch the **Settings** app and tap **Battery and device care** → **Storage**. Swipe leftwards to view the **SD card** page. Tap ⁝ and then **Format**.

CAUTION: Before you format the memory card, remember to make backup copies of all important data stored in the memory card. Loss of data resulting from user actions is not covered in the manufacturer's warranty.

Turning the device on and off

NOTE: Follow all posted warnings and directions from relevant authorities in areas where the use of wireless devices is restricted, such as aeroplanes and hospitals.

Volume Down key

Side key

Turning the device on

Press and hold the Side key for some seconds to turn on the device.

Turning the device off

1   To turn off the device, press and hold the Side key and the Volume Down key all at the same time. Alternatively, open the notification menu, swipe downwards, and then tap ⏻.

2   Tap **Power off**.

If you want to restart the device, tap **Restart**.

NOTE: You can configure the device to turn off when you press and hold the Side key. Go to the **Settings** app, click **Advanced features** → **Side key**, and then click **Power off menu** under **Press and hold**.

Forcing restart

If your device becomes frozen and unresponsive, press and hold the Side key and the Volume Down key simultaneously for a period longer than 7 seconds to restart it.

Emergency mode

You may switch the device to emergency mode to reduce battery consumption. Some apps and functions will be limited. In emergency mode, you can make an emergency call, send your current location information to others, sound an emergency alarm, etc. with your device.

To activate the Emergency mode in your device, press and hold the Side key and the Volume Down key simultaneously, then tap **Emergency mode**. Alternatively, you can open the notification panel, swipe downwards, and then tap ⏻ → **Emergency mode**.

To deactivate your device's emergency mode, tap ⋮ → **Turn off Emergency mode**.

NOTE: The usage time left displays the time remaining before the battery power runs out. Usage time left may differ depending on your device settings and operating circumstances.

CHAPTER TWO: HOW TO SET UP YOUR DEVICE

Initial setup

By then time you turn on your device for the first time or after performing a data reset, follow the on-screen instructions to set up your device.

NOTE: Unless you connect to a Wi-Fi network, you may not be able to set up some device features during the initial setup.

Samsung account

Your Samsung account is an integrated account service that lets you to use several of Samsung services offered by mobile devices, TVs, and the Samsung website.

To see the list of services that can be used with your Samsung account, please visit account.samsung.com.

1 Go to the **Settings** app, tap **Accounts and backup** → **Manage accounts** → **Add account** → **Samsung account**.

Or launch the **Settings** → **Samsung account**.

2 If you already have an existing Samsung account, sign in to your account.

- Click **Sign in with Google** to sign in using your Google account if you already have one.

- Click **Create account** to sign up if you do not have a Samsung account,

Finding your ID and resetting your password

If you ever forget your Samsung account ID or password, tap **Find ID** or **Forget password?** on the Samsung account sign-in screen. You'll be able to find your ID or reset your password after you enter the required information.

Signing out of your Samsung account

Any time you sign out of your Samsung account, your data, such as contacts or events, will also be removed from your device.

1 From your **Settings** menu, tap **Accounts and backup** → **Manage accounts**.

2 Click **Samsung account** → **My profile** and click **Sign out** at the bottom of the screen.

3 Tap **Sign out**, then input your Samsung account password, and tap **OK**.

Transferring data from your previous device (Smart Switch)

You can use Smart Switch to transfer data from your old device to your new device. Open the **Settings** app and tap **Accounts and backup → Bring data from old device**.
NOTE:

- This feature may not be available on some devices or computers.
- Restrictions apply. Please visit www.samsung.com/smartswitch for details. Samsung takes copyright as sacrosanct. You should only transfer content that you own or have the right to transfer.

Transferring data using a USB cable

You can connect your old device to your device with the USB cable to effortlessly and quickly transfer data.

1 Connect your device and the previous device using your device's USB cable. A USB connector may be needed depending on your old device.

2 When the app selection pop-up window displays, tap **Smart Switch → Receive data**.

3 In your old device, tap **Allow**.

If you do not have the app, download it from **Galaxy Store** or **Play Store**.

Your device will automatically recognize the previous device and display a list of data you can transfer.

4   Choose an item to bring and tap **Next** and follow the on-screen commands to complete transferring data.

CAUTION: Never disconnect the USB cable from the device when you are transferring files. Doing so may cause data loss or device damage.

NOTE: Transferring data increases the rate of battery power consumption by your device. Make sure your device is well charged before transferring data. Low battery power may cause interruption of data transfer.

Transferring data wirelessly

Transfer data from your previous device to your device wirelessly via Wi-Fi Direct by following the simple steps:

1   Launch **Smart Switch** on your previous device.

If you do not have the app in the device, download it from **Galaxy Store** or **Play Store**.

2   On your device, open the **Settings** app and tap **Accounts and backup** → **Bring data from old device**.

3   Place the devices close to each other.

4   On your old device, tap **Send data** → **Wireless**.

5 Still on the old device, tap **Allow**.

6 On your device, select an item to bring and tap **Next**. Follow the onscreen commands to complete transferring data.

Backing up and restoring data using external storage

Transfer data using external storage, such as a microSD (memory) card.

1 Back up data from your old device to external storage.

2 Insert or connect the external storage device to your device.

3 On your device, go to the **Settings** app and tap **Accounts and backup** → **External storage transfer**.

4 Choose the backup date under **Restore from SD card** and tap **Next**.

5 Follow the on-screen instructions to transfer data from external storage.

Transferring backup data from a computer

You can transfer data between your device and a computer. However, you must first of all download the Smart Switch computer version app from www.samsung.com/smarts-witch. You can also back up data from your previous device to a computer and import the data to your device.

1   Go to www.samsung.com/smartswitch on your computer to download Smart Switch.

2   On the computer, launch Smart Switch app.

NOTE: If your previous device is not a Samsung device, then you've to back up your data to a computer using a program provided by the device's manufacturer. Then, skip to the fifth step.

3   Now, connect your previous device to the computer using the device's USB cable.

4   Following the on-screen instructions on the computer, back up data from the device.

5.   Thereafter, disconnect your previous device from the computer.

6.   Now, connect your device to the computer using the USB cable.

7.   On the computer, follow the on-screen instructions in order to transfer data to your device.

Understanding the screen

Controlling the touchscreen

Tapping
Tap the screen.

Tapping and holding
Tap and hold the screen for approximately 2 seconds.

Dragging
Tap and hold an item and drag it to the target position.

Double-tapping
Double-tap the screen.

Swiping
Swipe upwards, downwards, to the left, or to the right.

Spreading and pinching
Spread two fingers apart or pinch on the screen.

CAUTION:

• Never allow the touchscreen to come into contact with other electrical devices. Electrostatic discharges can make the touchscreen to malfunction.

• To avoid damaging the touchscreen, do not tap it with anything sharp object, or apply any excessive pressure to it with your fingertips.

- It is recommended not to use fixed graphics on part or all of the touchscreen for prolonged periods as this may cause afterimages (screen burn-in) or ghosting.

NOTE:

The device may not be able to identify touch inputs close to the edges of the screen, which are not within the touch input area.

Navigation bar (soft buttons)

Any time you turn on the screen, the soft buttons will display on the navigation bar at the bottom of the screen. By default, the soft buttons are configured to the Recents button, Home button, and Back button from left to right respectively. The functions of the buttons can change depending on the app currently being used or operating environment.

Button		Function
|||	Recents	• Tap to open the list of recent apps.
O	Home	• Tap to return to the Home screen. • Tap and hold to launch the **Google Assistant** app.
❮	Back	• Tap to return to the previous screen.

Hiding the navigation bar

Hiding the navigation bar enables you to view files or use apps on a wider screen.

From the **Settings** app, tap **Display** → **Navigation bar**, and then tap **Swipe gestures** under **Navigation type**. The navigation bar will be hidden and the gesture hints will show up. Tap **More options** and select your desired option.

Swipe from bottom

Swipe from sides and bottom

28

If you like to hide the gesture hints at the bottom of the screen, tap the **Gesture hints** switch to deactivate it.

Home screen and Apps screen

The Home screen is the starting point from where you can access all of the features of your device. It shows widgets, shortcuts to apps, and much more.

The Apps screen displays icons for all apps installed on your device.

Switching between Home and Apps screens

To open the Apps screen, swipe the Home screen upwards. To return to the Home screen, swipe the Apps screen upwards or downwards; or instead, tap the Home button or the Back button.

If the Apps button has been added on the Home screen, you can open the Apps screen simply by tapping the button. To add it, follow the simple steps:

1. On the Home screen, tap and hold an empty area.

2. Tap **Settings**

3. Activate the **Show Apps screen button on Home screen** by tapping the switch.

The Apps button is straightaway added at the bottom of the Home screen.

Editing the Home screen

From the Home screen, tap and hold an empty area, or pinch your fingers together to view the editing options. Here, you can set the wallpaper; add widgets; and add, delete, or rearrange Home screen panels.

- To add panels, swipe to the left, and then tap ⊕.

- To move panels, tap and hold a panel preview, then drag it to a new location.

- To delete panels, tap 🗑 the panel.

- **Wallpapers and style**: You can change the wallpaper settings for the Home screen and the locked screen.

- **Themes**: You can change the device's theme. Note that visual elements of interface, such as colours, icons, and wallpapers, will change according to the selected theme.

- **Widgets**: These are small apps that launch specific app functions to give information and convenient access on your Home screen. Select a widget and tap **Add**. The widget will be added on the Home screen accordingly.

- **Settings**: Organize settings for the Home screen, such as the screen layout.

Displaying all apps on the Home screen

If you don't want to use a separate Apps screen, you can set the device to display all your apps on the Home screen. On the Home screen, just tap and hold an empty area, and then tap **Settings** → **Home screen layout** → **Home screen only** → **Apply**.

With that, you'll be able to access all your apps by swiping to the left on the Home screen.

Launching Finder

Quickly search for content on the device.

1. On the Apps screen, tap **Search**. Otherwise, open the notification panel and swipe downwards, then tap Q.

2. Type in a keyword. All the apps and content on your device will be searched.

You can search for more content by taping Q on the keyboard.

Moving items

1. Tap and hold an item

2. Drag it to a new location.

3. Drag it to the side of the screen if you want to move the item to another panel.

Adding a shortcut to an app on the Home screen:

1. Tap and hold an item on the Apps screen

2. Tap **Add to Home**.

If you like, you can also move frequently used apps to the shortcuts area at the bottom of the Home screen.

Creating folders

Create folders and collect related apps to quickly access and launch apps.

1. On the Home screen or the Apps screen, tap and hold an app

2. Drag the selected app over another app. A new folder comprising the selected apps will be created. 3. Tap **Folder name** and input a folder name.

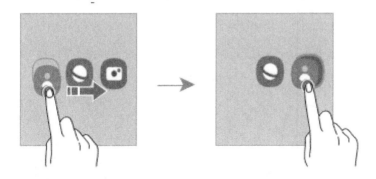

- **Adding more apps**

  Simply tap ✚ on the folder. Select the apps to add by ticking them and tap **Done**. Alternately, just drag the app you want to add to the folder.

- **Moving apps from a folder**

  Tap and hold an app if you want to drag it to a new location.

- **Deleting a folder**

  Tap and hold a folder, and then tap the **Delete folder**. Note that only the folder will be deleted. The apps in the folder will be relocated to the Apps screen.

Edge panel

The Edge panel enables you to quickly access your favourite apps and features.

Pull the Edge panel handle towards the centre of the screen. If the Edge panel handle is not visible on the screen, go to the **Settings** app, tap **Display**, and then tap the **Edge panels** switch to activate.

Edge panel

Edge

Edge panel settings

Lock screen

By pressing the Side key, you'll make the screen to turn off and lock. The screen will also turn off and automatically lock if the device is not used for a given period.

To unlock the screen, turn it on and swipe in any direction of the screen.

If the screen is off, press the Side key to turn it on or you double-click the screen.

Changing the screen lock method

To modify how the screen locks, launch the **Settings** app, tap **Lock screen** → **Screen lock type**, and then choose a method.

Setting a pattern, PIN, password, or your biometric data for the screen lock method protects your personal information by preventing others from having unauthorized access to your device. After setting the screen lock method, the device will require an unlock code anytime you want to unlock it.

NOTE: If you like your device to perform a factory data reset if you enter the unlock code incorrectly several times in a row and get to the attempt limit, Start the **Settings** app, click **Lock screen** → **Secure lock settings**, unlock the screen by using the preset screen lock method, and then click the **Auto factory reset** switch to activate it.

Indicator icons

Indicator icons will show on the status bar at the top of the screen. The icons shown in the table below are most commonly in use:

Icon	Meaning
⊘	No signal
,ıll	Signal strength
ᴿ,ıll	Roaming (outside of normal service area)
G ↓↑	GPRS network connected
E ↓↑	EDGE network connected
3G ↓↑	UMTS network connected

36

Icon	Meaning
H↓↑	HSDPA network connected
H+↓↑	HSPA+ network connected
4G↓↑ / **LTE**↓↑	LTE network connected
5G↓↑	5G network connected
Icon	**Meaning**
5G↓↑	Connected to LTE network with the 5G network
🛜	Wi-Fi connected
✺	Bluetooth feature activated
⦿	Location services being used
📞	Call in progress
⤣	Missed call
💬	New text or multimedia message
⏰	Alarm activated
🔇 / 🔇	Mute mode / Vibration mode
✈	Flight mode activated
⚠	Error occurred or caution required
🔋 / 🔋	Battery charging / Battery power level

NOTE:

- The status bar may not show at the top of the screen in some apps. To show the status bar, drag down from the top of the screen.

- Some indicator icons show only when you open the notification panel.

- The indicator icons may show separately based on the service provider or model.

Notification panel

Anytime you receive new notifications, indicator icons will show on the status bar. To see additional information about the icons, open the notification panel and view the details.

Quick setting buttons

Launch **Settings.**

Control connected nearby devices and SmartThings devices and scenes.

Control media on your device and connected nearby devices.

View the notification details and perform various actions.

Clear all notifications.

Access the notification settings.

Drag the status bar downwards to open the notification panel, and swipe upwards on the screen to close it.

38

The following functions on the notification panel commonly used:

Using quick setting buttons

Tap quick setting buttons to activate specific features. Swipe downwards on the notification panel to show you more buttons. To add more buttons, click ⊕

— Quick setting buttons

— Adjust the brightness of the display.

To change any feature settings, tap the text under each button. To view additional settings, tap and hold a button.

To rearrange buttons, tap ⋮ → **Edit buttons**, tap and hold a button, and then drag it to another location.

Controlling media playback

With the Media feature, you can take total control of your music or video playback. You can also continue playback on another device.

1. Open the notification panel and tap **Media**.
2. Tap the icons on the controller to take charge and control the playback.
3. To continue the playback on another device, touch ⓓ and pick the device you want.

Controlling nearby devices

Launch swiftly and be in control of nearby connected devices and frequently used SmartThings devices and scenes on the notification panel.

1 Open the notification panel and tap **Devices**.
Nearby connected devices and SmartThings devices and scenes will show up.

2 Select a nearby device or a SmartThings device to control it, or select a scene to launch it.

Screen capture and screen record

Screen capture

Feel like capturing a screenshot while using the device and lovingly write on, draw on, crop, or share the captured screen? Simple!

How to capture a screenshot

Use the following simple approaches to capture a screenshot. You'll be able to view the captured screenshots in **Gallery**.

Approach 1) Key capture: Press the Side key and the Volume Down key together at the same time.

Approach 2) Swipe capture: Swipe your hand to the left or right just across the device's screen.

NOTE:

- You'll not be able to capture a screenshot while using some apps and features.

- If capturing a screenshot by swiping is not yet activated in your device, launch the **Settings** app, tap **Advanced features → Motions and gestures**, and then tap the **Palm swipe to capture** switch to activate it.

After taking a screenshot, select from the following options on the toolbar at the bottom of the screen:

- [⌄] : Allows you to capture the current content and the hidden content on an extended page, such as a webpage. When you tap [⌄], the screen automatically scrolls down to capture more contents.

- ✐ : Enables you to write or draw on the screenshot or crop a section from the screenshot. You can then view the cropped area in **Gallery**.

- # : This will help you add some tags to the screenshot. To find screenshots by tag, tap **Search** just at the top of the Apps screen and tap **Screenshots** → Q. You can see the tags list and effortlessly find the screenshot you're looking for.

- ⦷ : Lets you share the screenshot with others.

NOTE: If you do not see the options on the captured screen, simply go to the **Settings** app, tap **Advanced features** → **Screenshots and screen recorder**, and then tap the **Screenshot toolbar** switch to activate it. And there you are!

42

Screen record

Would you like to record the screen while using your device? Follow the simple steps:

1. Open the notification panel,
2. Swipe downwards,
3. Tap 🔘 (**Screen recorder**) to activate it.
4. Choose a sound setting and tap **Start recording**. You'll have a countdown, after which recording will start.

    • If you want to write or draw on the screen, simply tap ✐.

5. After recording the video, tap ■ to stop.

Your video will be automatically saved in **Gallery**.

NOTE: To modify the screen recorder settings, launch the **Settings** app and tap **Advanced features** → **Screenshots and screen recorder**.

Entering text

Keyboard layout

A keyboard displays automatically when you enter text.

Additional keyboard functions — View more keyboard functions.

Enter uppercase. For all caps, tap it twice. — Delete a preceding character.

Enter symbols. — Break to the next line.

Enter a space.

NOTE: Not all languages support Text entry. To enter text, you must first of all change the input language to one that is supported.

Changing the input language

Tap ⚙ → **Languages and types** → **Manage input languages** and pick the languages to use. When you select two or more languages, you can switch from one input language to another by swiping to the left or right on the space key.

Changing the keyboard

Open the navigation bar, tap ⣿ to change the keyboard.

To change the keyboard type, tap ⚙ → **Languages and types**, pick a language, and then select the keyboard type you wish to use.

NOTE:

- If the keyboard button (⣿) does not show on the navigation bar, start the **Settings** app, click **General**

44

management → **Keyboard list and default**, and then click **Keyboard button on navigation bar** switch to activate the feature.

• On a **3 x 4** keyboard, a key comprises of three or four characters. To input a character, click the corresponding key repeatedly until the desired character appears.

Copying and pasting

1 Tap and hold over text.

2 Drag ⬤ ⬤ to the extent you wish to highlight the desired text, or tap **Select all** to select all text.

3 Click **Copy** or **Cut**.

The text you have highlighted will be copied to the clipboard.

4 Touch and hold where the text is to be pasted and click **Paste** to insert the copied text.

To paste text that you have

Additional keyboard functions

• ☺ : Enter emoticons.

• 🙂 : Enter stickers. You can also input your emoji stickers that look like you. See Using your emoji stickers in chats for more details.

• GIF : Attach animated GIFs.

- ⬤ : Enter text by voice.

- ⚙ : Change the keyboard settings.

Tap ••• to use more keyboard functions.

- Q : Search for content and enter it in.

- 🔤 : Translate text and enter it in.

- (Pass) : Type in your personal information registered to Samsung Pass.

- ▶ : Share video links.

- ⎙ : Add an item from the clipboard.

- ⟨↕⟩ : Open the text editing panel.

- ⌨ : Change the keyboard mode.

- ⬚ : Change the keyboard size.

- 😀 / 👧 / 💫 : Enter stickers.

NOTE: Some features may unavailable depending on the service provider or model.

CHAPTER THREE:
APPS AND FEATURES

Installing or uninstalling apps

Galaxy Store

Buy and download apps. You can download apps that are dedicated to Samsung Galaxy devices.

Launch the **Galaxy Store** app. Surf apps by category or tap Q to search for keywords.

NOTE:

- This app may not be present depending on the service provider or model.

- To modify the auto update settings, tap **Menu** → ⚙ ⇢ **Auto update apps**, and then select an option.

Play Store

Buy and download apps.

Launch the **Play Store** app. Surf apps by category or search for apps by keyword.

NOTE: To modify the auto update settings, tap the icon for your account, the go to **Settings** → **Network Preferences** → **Auto-update apps**, and then pick from the available options.

Managing apps

Uninstalling or disabling apps

Tap and hold an app and select from the options:

- **Uninstall**: Uninstall downloaded apps.

- **Disable**: Disable marked default apps that cannot be uninstalled from the device.

NOTE: Some apps may not function with this feature.

Enabling apps

Launch the **Settings** app, tap **Apps** → ↓̄ → **Disabled** → **OK**, pick an app, and then tap **Enable**.

Setting app permissions

For some apps to function well, they may request permission to access or use information on your device.

To see your app permission settings, launch the **Settings** app and tap **Apps**. Pick an app and tap **Permissions**. You can peruse the app's permissions list and change its permissions.

To display or modify app permission settings by permission category, launch the **Settings** app and tap **Apps** → ⋮ → **Permission manager**. Pick an item and pick an app.

NOTE: Unless you grant permissions to apps, the basic features of the apps may not work optimally.

Phone

Make/answer voice and video calls:

NOTE:

- If the part around the rear camera is covered, unwanted noises may be experienced during a call.
- Remove any accessories like screen protector and stickers close to the back camera.

Making calls

1. Open the **Phone** app and tap **Keypad**.

2. Enter a phone number.

3. Tap 📞 to make a voice call, or tap 📹 or 📹 you want to make a video call.

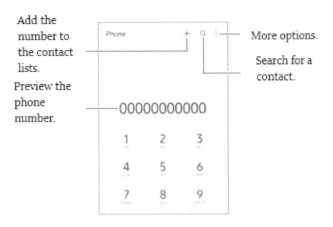

Add the number to the contact lists.

Preview the phone number.

More options.

Search for a contact.

Making calls from call logs or contacts list

Open the **Phone** app, tap **Recents** or **Contacts**, and then swipe to the right on a contact or a phone number to make a call.

If this feature is not activated, tap **⋮** → **Settings** → **Other call settings**, followed by a tap on **Swipe to call or text** switch to activate it.

Using speed dial

To assign a number to speed dial, open the **Phone** app, tap **Keypad** or **Contacts** → **⋮** → **Speed dial numbers**, pick a speed dial number, after which you add a phone number.

To make a call, simply click and hold a speed dial number on the keypad. For speed dial numbers from 10 upwards, click the first digit(s) of the number, and then tap and hold the last digit.

For example, if you set the number **456** as a speed dial number, tap **4**, tap **5**, and then tap and hold **6**.

Making an international call

1 Open the **Phone** app and click **Keypad**.

2 Touch and hold **0** until it changes to the plus (+) sign .

3 Type in the country code, area code, and phone number, and then tap 📞.

Receiving calls

Answering a call

When you have an incoming call, drag 📞 outside the large circle to receive the call.

Rejecting a call

When you have an incoming call, drag ☎ outside the large circle to reject the call.

If you wish to send a message when rejecting an incoming call, drag the **Send message** bar upwards and choose a message to send.

To create different rejection messages, open the **Phone** app, tap ⋮ → **Settings** → **Quick decline messages**, type a message, and then tap ✛.

Blocking phone numbers

Block calls from precise numbers added to your block list.

1   Open the **Phone** app and tap $\vdots$ → **Settings** → **Block numbers**.

2   Tap **Recents** or **Contacts**, pick the contacts or phone numbers, and then tap **Done**. To manually enter a number, tap **Add phone number**, type in a phone number, and then tap ┼.

When blocked numbers attempt to reach you, you will not receive notifications. You will find the calls in the call log.

NOTE:

If you like to block incoming calls from people who hide their caller ID, just tap the **Block unknown/private numbers** switch to activate the feature.

Options during calls

*   **Add call**: you can dial a second call while making a call. The first call will be placed on hold. When you end the second call, the first call will resume.

*   **Hold call**: Place a call on hold.

*   **Bluetooth**: Shift to a Bluetooth headset if it is connected to the device.

- **Speaker**: You may wish to activate or deactivate the speakerphone. When you are using the speakerphone, do not keep the device close to your ears.

- **Mute**: When you turn off the microphone, the other party will not be able to hear you.

- **Keypad/Hide**: Open or close keypad.

- ⬤ : Tap ⬤ to end the current call.

- **Camera**: During a video call, if you turn off the camera, the other party cannot see you.

- **Switch**: During a video call, you can switch between the front and back cameras.

NOTE: Some features may be restricted depending on the service provider or model.

Contacts

You are able to create new contacts or manage contacts on the device.

Adding contacts

Creating a new contact

1 Open the **Contacts** app and tap ✛.

2 Pick a storage location.

3 input contact information and tap **Save**.

Importing contacts

You may also like to add contacts by importing them from other storage media to your device.

1 Open the **Contacts** app and click ☰ → **Manage contacts** → **Import or export contacts** → **Import**.

2 Follow the instructions that display on the screen to import contacts.

Syncing contacts with your web accounts

you can set your device contacts to synchronize with online contacts saved in your web accounts, such as your Samsung account. Just follow the simple steps:

1 Open the **Settings** app, tap **Accounts and backup** → **Manage accounts** and choose the account to sync with.

2 Tap **Sync account** and tap the **Contacts** switch to get it activated.

Searching for contacts

Open the **Contacts** app. Tap Q at the top of the contacts menu and enter search criteria.

Tap the contact, and then take an action from the following options:

- 📞 : Make a voice call.

- 📹 / 📹 : Make a video call.

- 💬 : Compose a message.

- 📧 : Compose an email.

Deleting contacts

1 Open the **Contacts** app and tap ⋮ → **Delete contacts**.

2 Pick contacts and tap **Delete**.

To delete contacts one by one, tap a contact from the contacts menu and tap **More** → **Delete**.

Sharing contacts

You can your share contacts with others by using several sharing options:

1 Open the **Contacts** app and tap ⋮ → **Share contacts**.

2 Choose contacts and tap **Share**.

3 Decide a sharing method.

Creating groups

If you like to add groups, such as family or friends, and manage contacts by group, follow these steps:

1 Open the **Contacts** app and tap ☰ → **Groups** → **Create group**.

2 Follow the on-screen directives to create a group.

Merging duplicate contacts

If you have duplicated contacts in your list, merge them into one to update your contacts list.

1   Open the **Contacts** app and tap $\equiv$ → **Manage contacts** → **Merge contacts**.

2   Tick contacts and tap **Merge**.

Messages

Send and view messages by conversation.

You may need to pay additional charges for sending or receiving messages while roaming.

Sending messages

1 Open the **Messages** app and tap ⊙.

2 Add recipients and enter a message.

If you like to record and send a voice message, tap and hold 'ıll', say your message, and then release your finger from the icon. The recording icon will only appear when the message input field is empty.

3 Tap ⊘ to send the message.

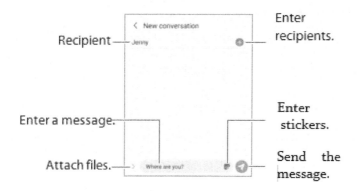

Recipient — [diagram label]
Enter recipients.
Enter a message.
Enter stickers.
Attach files.
Send the message.

Viewing messages

1. Open the **Messages** app and tap **Conversations**.

2. On the message menu, pick a contact or a phone number.

- If you're replying to the message, tap the message input field, enter a message, and then tap send [].

- To adjust the font size, drag two fingers apart or pinch on the screen.

Sorting messages

You can sort messages by category and manage them without stress.

Open the **Messages** app and tap **Conversations** and tap the plus sign (+) to add category.

If the category option does not show, tap ⋮ → **Settings** and tap the **Conversations categories** switch for it to be activated.

Deleting messages

Just tap and hold a message to delete, then tap **Delete**.

Changing message settings

Mount the **Messages** app, tap ⁝ → **Settings**. Here, you can also block unwanted messages, change notification settings, and so on.

Internet

Here, browsing the Internet to search for information and bookmarking your favourite webpages to access them is fun.

1   Launch the **Internet** app.

2   Type in the web address or a keyword, and then tap **Go**. For you to view the toolbars, just drag your finger downwards a little on the screen.

If you want to switch between tabs swiftly, swipe to the left or right on the address field.

Bookmark the current webpage.

Refresh the current webpage.

View you bookmarks.

Open the homepage.

Manage taps. / User secret mode.

Move between pages.

More options

Using secret mode

You can prevent others from viewing your search history, browsing history, bookmarks, and saved pages by setting a password for secret mode.

1 Touch ☖ → **Turn on Secret mode**.

2 Touch the **Lock Secret mode** switch to activate it, touch **Start**, and then set a password for secret mode.

In secret mode, the device will normally change the colour of the toolbars. Anytime you want to deactivate secret mode, touch ⬚ → **Turn off Secret mode**.

NOTE: In secret mode, some features, such as screen capture may not be available.

CHAPTER FOUR:

THE CAMERA AND GALLERY APPS

Camera

Capture pictures and record videos with various modes and settings.

Camera etiquette

- Do not take pictures or record videos of other people unless they have permitted you to do so.

- Do not take pictures or record videos in places where it is legally forbidden.

- Do not take pictures or record videos in places where your action may result in violation of other people's privacy.

Taking pictures

1. Open the **Camera** app.

   You can also launch the app by pressing the Side key twice quickly or by dragging the camera icon () to the left on the locked screen.

2. Touch the image on the preview screen where you want the camera to focus.

- To adjust the brightness of pictures, pull the adjustment bar that displays above or below the circular frame.

3 Tap ◯ to take a picture.

- To alter the shooting mode, pull the shooting modes list to the left or right, or swipe either to the left or right on the preview screen.

Camera settings

Options for current shooting mode

Zoom

Scene optimizer

Preview thumbnail

Shooting mode list

Take a picture

Switch between the front and rear cameras

NOTE:

- Some features of the camera are absent when you launch the **Camera** app from the locked screen or when the screen is turned off if your device has its screen lock method set.

- The camera automatically shuts off when it's not in use.

- Some methods may be absent depending on the service provider or model.

- The preview screen may differ based on the shooting mode and the type of camera being used.

- High resolution and high zoom ratio decrease the clarity of pictures and videos when taken from a close range. Therefore, maintain a good distance when taking pictures or videos.

- If you take pictures and they appear blurry, clean the camera lens and try taking again.

- Ensure that the lens is never damaged or contaminated. Or else, the device may not work well in some modes requiring high resolutions.

- Your device's camera possesses a wide-angle lens. Slight alteration may occur in wide-angle pictures or videos and does not imply device performance problems. To correct any alteration in pictures, tap ⚙ on the preview screen, touch **Format and advanced options**, and then touch the **Ultra wide shape correction** switch to make it activated.

- The highest capacity for video recording may differ depending on the resolution.

- If the device is exposed to sudden changes in air temperature, the camera may fog up or form condensation as a result of the difference in temperature outside and inside the camera cover. Take caution to avoid such conditions when planning to use the camera. If fogging occurs, allow the camera to dry naturally at room temperature before taking pictures or recording videos, otherwise results may look blurry.

Using zoom features

Choose **.5/1/2** or pull it to the left or right to zoom in or out. Alternatively, drag your two fingers apart on the screen to zoom in, and tweak to zoom out.

NOTE:

- **.5**: The Ultra-wide camera allows you to take wide-angle pictures or record wide-angle videos of things such as landscapes.

- **1**: The wide-angle camera allows you to take basic pictures or record normal simple videos.

- **2**: The telephoto camera enables you to take pictures or record videos by increasing the subject size.

You can only make use of the zoom features when using the rear camera.

Locking the focus (AF) and exposure (AE)

You can lock the focus or exposure on a selected portion to inhibit the camera from automatically adjusting based on changes to the subjects or light sources.

Tap and hold the portion to focus, the AF/AE frame will display on the portion and the focus and exposure setting will be locked. The setting will still remain locked even after you take a picture.

NOTE: The availability of this feature is subject to the shooting mode.

Using the camera button

- Touch and hold the camera button to record a video.
- If you like to take burst shots, simply swipe the camera button to the edge of the screen and hold it.

65

- If you've added another camera button, you can move it anywhere on the screen and take pictures more handily. On the preview screen, touch ⚙ → **Shooting methods** and touch the **Floating Shutter button** switch to activate it.

Options for current shooting mode

On the preview screen, make use of the following options:

- ⚡ : To activate or deactivate the flash.

- ⓞFF : Choose how long to delay before the camera automatically takes a picture.

- 3:4 : Choose an aspect ratio and resolution for your pictures.

- ⓘ : To activate or deactivate the motion photo feature. If this feature is activated, a video clip will also be taken from a few seconds before tapping the camera button.

- ✋ : To activate or deactivate the super steady feature to calm a video.

- Cᴀ : To pick a frame rate.

- 3:4 : To choose an aspect ratio for videos.

- **FHD** 30 : To choose a resolution for videos.
- ☀ : To apply any filter effect or beauty effects.
- ◎ : To choose a metering method. This controls how light values are calculated. ◎ **Centre-weighted** makes use of the light in the centre portion of the shot to determine the exposure of the shot. **(○) Spot** makes use of the light in a concentrated centre portion of the shot to determine the exposure of the shot. **(◇) Matrix** takes the average the entire scene.
- ⬤ : In **FOOD** mode, instructing to focus on a subject within the circular frame and blur the image outside the frame.
- ✹ : In **FOOD** mode, instructing to regulate the colour tone.

NOTE: The options available may differ according to the model or shooting mode.

Photo mode

The camera regulates the shooting options automatically based on the immediate surroundings to capture pictures easily.

From the shooting modes menu, tap **PHOTO** and tap ○ to take a picture.

67

Taking high-resolution pictures

Take high-resolution pictures following these simple steps: In the shooting options, tap **3:4**, then **3:4 64MP** and take a picture.

NOTE: If this feature has not been activated, tap ⚙ on the preview screen and tap the **Scene optimizer** switch to activate it.

Shot suggestions

The camera recommends the ideal composition for the picture by identifying the position and angle of your subject.

On the preview screen, click ⚙ and touch the **Shot suggestions** switch to activate it.

1. On the shooting modes list, click **PHOTO**.

   A guide will display on the preview screen.

2. Point the guide directly at the subject.

   The camera will recognize the composition, and the recommended composition will display on the preview screen.

3. Move the device around until the guide matches the recommended composition.

   When the ideal composition is attained, the guide will change its colour to yellow.

4 Tap ◯ to take a picture.

Ideal composition

Guid

Taking selfies

You can take self-portraits with the front camera of your device.

1 On the preview screen, swipe upwards or downwards, or click ◉ to switch to the front camera for self-portraits.

2. Face the front camera lens.

If you want to take self-portraits with a wide-angle shot of the landscape or people, click ⊙.

3 Click ◯ to take a picture.

Applying filter and beauty effects

You can choose a filter effect and alter facial features, such as your skin tone or face shape, before actually taking a picture.

1 On the preview screen, click ✳.

2 Choose effects and take a picture.

If you're using the My filters style, you can create your own filter by using an image with a colour tone you love from the **Gallery**.

Video mode

The camera will adjust the shooting options automatically in relation on the surroundings to record videos easily.

1 On the shooting modes menu, click **VIDEO** and click ⊙ to record a video.

   • To switch from the front to the rear camera and vice versa while recording, swipe upwards or downwards on the preview screen or click ⊙. (SM-A526B)

   • To snap an image from the video while recording, click ⊚.

2 Tap ▉ to stop recording the video.

Stabilizing videos (Super steady)

This feature enables you to stabilize videos when recording.

To use the feature, simply tap **VIDEO** on the shooting modes menu, activate it by tap ⫯ on the shooting options, and afterwards, record a video.

Portrait mode

The camera enables you to take shots where the background is blurred and the subject stands out clearly.

1   Tap **PORTRAIT** from the shooting modes menu.

2   Move the background blur adjustment bar to adjust the blur level.

3   As soon as you see **Ready** display on the preview screen, tap the capture button (◯) to take a picture.

Background blur adjustment bar

NOTE:

·   This feature is best used in a place with sufficient light.

·   The background blur may be poorly applied due to the following conditions:

- The device or the subject is moving.
- The subject is thin or transparent.
- The subject has a similar colour to the background.
- The subject or background is plain.

Fun mode

Take a picture with numerous effects.

On the shooting modes list, click **FUN**.

To choose a different effect, slide the camera button to the left or right.

Pro mode / Pro video mode

Capture pictures or videos as you manually adjust different shooting options, such as exposure value and ISO value.

From the shooting modes menu, click **MORE** → **PRO** or **PRO VIDEO**. Choose options and customize the settings, and then click ⚙ to take a picture or click ⊙ to record a video.

Available options

⟳   : Reset the settings.

ISO   : Choose an ISO value. This regulates camera light sensitivity. Smaller ISO values are used for stationary or well luminous objects. Higher values are used for fast-moving objects or objects with poor illumination. Nevertheless, higher ISO settings can cause noise in pictures or videos.

SPEED : Regulate the shutter speed. A slow shutter speed lets more light in, so the picture or video becomes brighter. This is perfect for pictures or videos of scenery or pictures or videos taken at night. A fast shutter speed lets less light in. This is perfect for capturing pictures or videos of fast-moving subjects.

EV : Change the exposure value. This controls how much light the camera's sensor receives. For low-light occasions, use a higher exposure.

FOCUS: Change the focus mode. Move the adjustment bar towards or to adjust the focus by yourself to satisfaction.

WB : Select a suitable white balance, to make your images have a true-to-life colour range. You can also set the colour temperature.

Separating the focus area and the exposure area

It is possible to separate the focus area and the exposure area.

Click and hold the preview screen. The AF/AE frame will display on the screen. Move the frame to the place where you want to separate the focus area and the exposure area.

Single take mode

Take different pictures and videos in just a single shot.

Your device automatically selects the best shot and generates pictures with filters or videos with certain segments repeated.

1   From the shooting modes list, click **MORE**, then **SINGLE TAKE**.

2   Click ◯ and move the camera to capture the scene you like to capture.

3   When you're done, click the preview thumbnail.
    To look at other results, move the ▬con upwards. If you like to save the results separately, click **Select** mark the items you want, and then click ⤓.

Customize the shooting options.

Night mode

Take a picture in low-light environment, without using the flash. When you use a tripod, you can get better results.

1 From the shooting modes menu, tap **MORE → NIGHT**.

2 Click ◯ and hold your device stable until shooting is complete.

Food mode

You can capture pictures of food with more lively colours.

1. From the shooting modes menu, click **MORE → FOOD**.

2. Touch the screen and pull the circular frame over the area to highlight.

The area outside the circular frame will be hazy.

To resize the circular frame, move a corner of the frame.

75

3. Tap   and move the adjustment bar to adjust the colour tone.

4. Click $\bigcirc$ to take a picture.

Panorama mode

You can take a series of pictures and then stitch them together to create a wide scene using the panorama mode.

1. From the shooting modes menu, click **MORE** → **PANORAMA**.

2. Click ⚭ and move the device slowly in one direction.

Retain the image inside the frame on the camera's viewfinder. If the preview image is not inside the guide frame or you don't move the device, the device will automatically cease to take pictures.

3. Click ⊙ to stop taking pictures.

NOTE: It's not advisable taking pictures of indistinct backgrounds, like an empty sky or a plain wall.

Macro mode

Allows you to pictures of subjects at close range.

From the shooting modes menu, click **MORE** → **MACRO**.

Super Slow-mo mode

Super slow motion is a feature that enables you to record a fast passing moment slowly so that you can appreciate it later.

1   From the shooting modes menu, click **MORE → SU-PER SLOW-MO** and click ⊚ to record a video. The device will record the instance in super slow motion and save it as a video.

2   From the preview screen, click the preview thumbnail and click **Play super slow-mo video**. If you want to edit the super slow motion section, tap ⋮ → **Editor** and shift the section editing bar to the left or right.

NOTE: Use this feature in an environment that has enough light. When recording a video indoors with inadequate or poor lighting, the screen may appear dark or be gritty. The screen may glimmer in certain lighting situations, such as in areas with fluorescent lighting.

Slow motion mode

Record a video to view it in slow motion. You can stipulate segments of your videos to be played in slow motion.

1. From the shooting modes menu, tap **MORE** → **SLOW MOTION** and tap to record a video.

2. When you are done recording, tap ⏺ to stop.

3. On the preview screen, click the preview thumbnail and click **Play slow motion video**.

> The fast segment of the video will be set as a slow-motion segment and the video will start playing. Up to two slow motion segments will be created according to the video.
>
> To edit the slow-motion segment, click ⋮ → **Editor** and move the segment editing bar to the left or right.

Super slow-mo-tion section

Start bracket

Section editing bar

End bracket

Hyperlapse mode

This feature enables you to record scenes, like passing people or cars, and view them as fast-motion videos.

78

1. On the shooting modes menu, click **MORE** → **HYPER-LAPSE**.

2. Tap Ⓒ and pick a frame rate option.

   If you set the frame rate to Ⓒ, that is **Auto**, the device will automatically regulate the frame rate depending on the changing rate of the scene.

3. Tap ◉ to start recording.

4. Tap ⦿ to complete recording.

Customizing camera settings

On the preview screen, click ◊ . Some options may be unavailable based on the shooting mode.

Intelligent features

- **Scene optimizer**: Helps to adjust the colour settings and apply the optimized effect automatically according to the subject or scene.

- **Shot suggestions**: Helps to suggest the perfect composition for the picture by identifying the position and angle of your subject.

- **Scan QR codes**: Enables the device to scan QR codes from the preview screen.

Pictures

- **Swipe Shutter button to**: Choose what happens when you swipe the camera button to the edge of the screen and hold it.

- **Format and advanced options**: choose how you want to save pictures.

  - **HEIF pictures**: Capture images in the High Efficiency Image Format (HEIF).

  - **Ultra wide shape correction**: Set the device to correct distortion in images captured with the Ultra wide camera.

Selfies

- **Use wide angle for group selfies**: Configure the device to automatically change to a wide-angle selfie when there are more than two people in the frame.

- **Save selfies as previewed**: Configure the device to save images as they appear on the preview screen when captured with the front camera without flipping them.

Videos

- **High efficiency videos**: Record your videos in the High Efficiency Video Codec (HEVC) format. Your HEVC videos will be saved as compressed files to help you manage the device's memory.

NOTE:

- You will not be able to play the HEVC videos on other devices or share them online.

- You will not be able to record Super slow motion and slow motion videos in the HEVC format.

- **Video stabilization**: Activate anti-shake to minimize or eliminate blurry image ensuing from camera shake while recording a video.

General

- **Auto HDR**: Capture images with rich colours and replicate details even in bright and dark areas.

- **Grid lines**: Show viewfinder guides to help composition when selecting subjects.

- **Location tags**: Attach a GPS location tag to the image.

  NOTE:

- GPS signal strength may reduce in places where the signal is obstructed, such as between buildings or in low-lying areas, or in poor weather conditions.

- Your location may show on your pictures when you upload them to the Internet. To prevent this, deactivate the location tag setting.

- **Shooting methods**: Select several more shooting methods for capturing an image or recording a video.

- **Settings to keep**: Preserve the last settings you used, such as the shooting mode, when you mount the camera.

- **Storage location**: Choose the memory location for storage. This feature will display when you insert a memory card.

- **Watermark**: Add a watermark at the bottom left corner of the screen when taking pictures.

- **Show Snapchat Licenses in Fun mode**: Automate the device to capture a photo with different effects with special unique Snapchat Lenses.

Privacy

- **Privacy Notice**: View the privacy notice.

- **Permissions**: View the permissions needed to operate the Camera app.

- **Reset settings**: Reset the camera settings

- **Contact us**: Ask questions or see frequently asked questions.

- **About Camera**: Check the Camera app version and legal information.

Please note that some features may not show depending on the model.

Gallery

Here, you can explore images and videos stored in your device. You can also manage images and videos according to album or create stories.

Using Gallery

Start the **Gallery** app.

Grouping similar images

Open the **Gallery** app and click to group similar images and show only the best shots as a preview of the images.

When you click the image preview, you'll be able to see all the images in the group.

Viewing images

Open the **Gallery** app and pick an image. To see other files, swipe to the left or right on the screen.

Bixby Vision

View the content on a large screen using the Smart View feature.

Modify the image.

Add the image to favourites.

Share the image with others.

Image and video thumbnail

More options

Delete the image.

Cropping enlarged images

1. Open the **Gallery** app and choose an image.

2. Drag two fingers apart on the area you want to save and click .

The cropped area will be saved for you as a file.

Saved
image
thumbnail

Viewing videos

Open the **Gallery** app and select a video to play. To view your other files, swipe to the left or right on the screen. To make use of several other options during playback, tap ⋮ , then tap **Open in Video player**.

View the content on a large screen using the Smart View feature.

Capture the current screen.

Switch to the pop-up video player.

Lock the playback screen.

Rewind or fast-forward by dragging the bar.

Skip to the previous video. Tap and hold to rewind.

Configure the caption settings.

More options

Create an animated GIF.

Change the screen ratio.

Rotate the screen.

Skip to the next video. Tap and hold to fast-forward.

Pause and resume playback.

move your finger up or down on the left side of the playback screen to regulate the brightness, or move your finger up or down on the right side of the playback screen to regulate the volume. To rewind or fast-forward, swipe to the left hand or right hand side on the playback screen.

Albums

Create albums and sort your images and videos.

1   Open the **Gallery** app and then tap **Albums** → ⋮ → **Create album** to create an album.

2   Select the album, click **Add items**, and then copy or move the images or videos you want.

Stories

Any time you capture or save images and videos, the device will read their date and location tags, sort the images and videos, and then create stories.

Open the **Gallery** app, tap **Stories**, and then select a story.

To add or delete images or videos, choose a story and tap ◊ → **Add** or **Edit**.

Syncing images and videos

Open the **Gallery** app, click ☰ → **Settings** → **Cloud sync**, and then follow the on-screen instructions to finish the sync. The **Gallery** app will be synced with the cloud.

When your **Gallery** app is synced with the cloud, your pictures and videos will also be saved in the cloud. You can view images and videos saved in the cloud in your **Gallery** app and from other devices any time.

NOTE: When you have your Samsung account and Microsoft account connected, you can set the cloud storage as Microsoft OneDrive.

Deleting images or videos

Open the **Gallery** app, touch and hold an image, a video, or a story to delete, and then click **Delete**.

Using the recycle bin feature

Reserve the deleted images and videos in the recycle bin. The files will be deleted after a given period.

Open the **Gallery** app, click ☰ → **Settings**, and then click the **Recycle bin** switch to activate it.

To view files in the recycle bin, open the **Gallery** app and click ☰ → **Recycle bin**.

AR Zone

Introduction

AR Zone offers you AR related features. Choose a feature and capture exciting pictures or videos.

Launching AR Zone

Use the following procedures to launch AR Zone:

• Open the **AR Zone** app.

- Open the **Camera** app and tap **MORE** → **AR ZONE**.

NOTE: Some features may be unavailable depending on the service provider or model.

AR Emoji Studio

Creating AR Emoji

Create an emoji that looks like you.

1   Open the **AR Zone** app and click **AR Emoji Camera** → ⊕.

2   Position your face straight on the screen, tap ○ and take a picture or tap **Make from pic** to choose a picture.

If you click **Pre-made emojis**, you can choose an emoji and decorate it any way you want.

3   Follow the on-screen guidelines to create an emoji.

Deleting an emoji

Open the **AR Zone** app and click **AR Emoji Studio**, tick the emoji you want to delete, and then click 🗑 **Delete**.

Making an AR emoji short video and using it to decorate your device

You may utilize an emoji as a wallpaper or call background picture by making a short movie with it.

1 To access AR Emoji Studio, open the **AR Zone** app and select **AR Emoji Studio**.

2 Choose from three options: **Create video, Call screen**, or **Lock screen**.

3 Choose a template that you wish to use.

To change the background image, press .

4 To save the video, tap **Save**.

In the **Gallery**, you may see the videos you've saved.

5 Choose an option at the bottom of the screen to utilize the video immediately.

Using an AR emoji to create your contact profile

Use an emoji as your Samsung account's profile image and in the **Contacts** app. You may select from a variety of postures or make your own.

1 Open the **AR Zone** app and select **AR Emoji Studio** from the menu.

2 Go to Profile and choose an emoji.

3 Tap to record your emotion or to choose a position.

4 Save by tapping **Done**.

Capturing pictures or videos with emojis

Create fun pictures or videos with emojis using different shooting modes.

1   Open the **AR Zone** app and click **AR Emoji Camera**.

2   Choose the emoji and the mode you want to use. The available modes may differ according to the emoji you choose.

- **SCENE**: The emoji will mimic your expressions.

- **MASK**: The emoji's face will appear over your face, making it look like you're wearing a mask.

- **MIRROR**: The emoji will mimic your body movements.

- **PLAY**: The emoji will move on a real background.

3   Click the emoji icon to capture a picture, or click and hold the icon to record a video.

You can view and share the pictures and videos that you have captured in tour device's **Gallery**.

AR Emoji Stickers

Make your own stickers with your emoji's expressions and actions. You will be able to use your emoji stickers when sending messages or use them on a social network.

Creating your own stickers

1 Open the **AR Zone** app and click **AR Emoji Stickers**.

2 Click **Make custom stickers** at the bottom of the screen.

3 Edit stickers as you like and click **Save**.

   You can view the stickers you have made by clicking **Custom**.

Deleting emoji stickers

Open the **AR Zone** app and click **AR Emoji Stickers** → **⋮** → **Delete stickers**. Choose the emoji stickers to delete and clcik **Delete**.

Using your emoji stickers in chats

You can use your emoji stickers when having a conversation through messages or on a social network. The underlisted actions are an example of using your emoji stickers in the **Messages** app.

1 During a message composition in the **Messages** app, click ☺ on the Samsung keyboard.

2   Tick the emoji icon.

3   Choose any of your emoji stickers.

    The emoji sticker will be put in.

Emoji icon

AR Doodle

Record fun videos with virtual handwriting or drawings on faces or any other part. As soon as the camera recognizes a face or space, the doodles on the face will then follow the face as it moves, and the doodles in the space will be fixed in the same place notwithstanding whether the camera moves.

1   Open the **AR Zone** app and tap **AR Doodle**.

    When the camera recognizes the subject, the recognition area will display on the screen.

2   Write or draw in the recognition area by tapping 🖊.

    • If you switch to the back camera, you can also write or draw outside the recognition area.

- If you tap ⊙ and then start doodling, you can record yourself doodling.

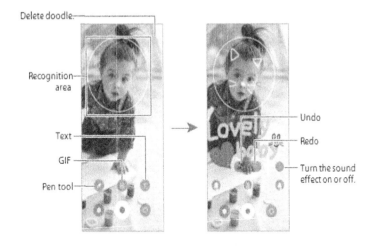

3. Tap ⊙ to record a video.

4. Tap ⊡ to stop recording the video.

You can view and share the video in your **Gallery**.

NOTE: The particular features displayed on the preview screen depend on the camera that's in use.

Deco Pic

Capture pictures or videos with different types of stickers.

Open the **AR Zone** app and tap **Deco Pic**.

CHAPTER FIVE: BIXBY

Introduction

Bixby is a user interface that enables you use your device more effortlessly.

You can either talk to Bixby or type text and it will initiate a function you request or show the information you want. Visit www.samsung.com/bixby for additional information.

NOTE:

Bixby is not available in all languages and regions.

Starting Bixby

Press and hold down the Side key to launch Bixby. The Bixby intro page will display. Choose the language you want to use with Bixby, then sign in to your Samsung account, and complete the setup following the on-screen instructions. Thereafter, the Bixby screen will display.

Using Bixby

While pressing and holding the Side key, say what you want to Bixby, and then release your finger from the key when you are done speaking. Instead, you can say "Hi, Bixby" and then say what you want to say.

For example, while pressing and holding the Side key, say "How's the weather today?" The weather information will display on the screen.

If you want to know tomorrow's weather:

1. Press and hold the Side key,

2. And say "Tomorrow?"

If Bixby asks you a question while having a conversation, here's what to do:

1. Press and hold the Side key and answer Bixby.

Or

2. Tap 🎤 and answer Bixby.

How about if you're using headphones or Bluetooth audio devices, or initiate a conversation by saying "Hi, Bixby"? Then you can continue the conversation without tapping the icon. Jus launch the **Bixby** app and tap ⊘ → ⋮ →

Settings → **Automatic listening** → **Hands-free only.**

Waking up Bixby using your voice

You can begin a conversation with Bixby by saying "Hi, Bixby". You'll have to register your voice so that Bixby will respond to your voice whenever you say "Hi, Bixby".

1   Open the **Bixby** app and tap ⊘   ⁝→   →

Settings → **Voice wake-up**.

2   Click the **Wake with "Hi, Bixby"** switch to activate it.

3   Activate it by clicking the **Recognize voice** switch.

4   Complete the setup by following the on-screen instructions.

Now you can say "Hi, Bixby" and begin a conversation.

Communicating by typing text

If your voice is not recognized as a result of noisy environments or if you are in a situation where you are having difficulty speaking, you can communicate with Bixby through text.

Open the **Bixby** app, tap ⌨, and then type what you want. Throughout the communication process, Bixby also will reply you through text instead of voice feedback.

Bixby Vision

Introduction

Bixby Vision is a service that offers different features according to image recognition. You can use Bixby Vision to search for information fast by just recognizing objects. Use several useful Bixby Vision features.

NOTE:

- The image size, format, or resolution can affect the availability of this feature as well as its accuracy in getting search results.
- Samsung is not accountable for the product information provided by Bixby Vision.

Launching Bixby Vision

Launch Bixby Vision using any of these procedures.

- In the **Camera** app, click **MORE** on the shooting modes menu and click **BIXBY VISION**.
- In the **Gallery** app, pick an image and click ⊙.
- In the **Internet** app, touch and hold an image and click **Search with Bixby Vision**.
- If you have the Bixby Vision app icon added to the Apps screen, launch the **Bixby Vision** app.

Using Bixby Vision

1 Launch Bixby Vision.

2 Choose a feature you want to use.

- (T) : Recognize text from documents or images and translate it.
- (Q) : Search for images resembling the recognized object online and related information.

- ⊕ : Search for information of products.

- ⊞ : Recognize QR codes and view information.

NOTE: The available features and search results may differ according to the region or service provider.

Bixby Routines

Introduction

Add your repeated usage patterns as routines and use your device more freely.

For example, a 'before bed' routine will perform such actions as turning on silent mode and dark mode, to not be vibrating on your eyes and ears when you use the device before going to bed.

Adding routines

1   Open the **Settings** app and click **Advanced features** → **Bixby Routines**.

2   On the **Discover** list, choose a routine you want or click **Add routine** to add your own routines.

- You can set the conditions and actions of routines on the **Discover** menu.

- If you want to program the routine's running condition to manual, click **Start manually**. This option will show only when there are no running conditions programmed. When a pop-up window displays, click **Add**. You can add the routine to the Home screen as a widget to quickly access it.

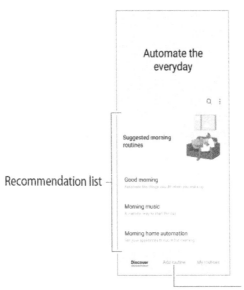

Recommendation list

Add your own routines.

Using routines

Running auto routines

Auto routines will run automatically whenever their conditions are detected.

Running manual routines

For manual routines which you programmed the running condition as **Start manually**, you can run them manually by clicking the button whenever you want.

Open the **Settings** app and click **Advanced features** →

Bixby Routines → **My routines** and click ▶ next to the

routine you want to run. Or instead, click the routine's

widget on the Home screen.

Viewing running routines

Routines that are currently will show on the notification

panel. To view a routine's details, click the notification.

You can also quickly terminate running routines. On the no-

tification panel, click ▼ next to a routine and click **Stop**.

Managing routines

Open the **Settings** app and click **Advanced features** →

Bixby Routines → **My routines**. Your routines will dis-

play.

To deactivate a routine, click the routine → **More** → **Disa-**

ble this routine.

To delete routines, click ⋮ → **Delete**, tick routines to delete,

and then click **Delete**.

Multi window

Introduction

Multi window allows you run two apps simultaneously in

the split screen view. You can also run multiple apps simul-

taneously in the pop-up view.

Split screen view   Pop-up view

NOTE: Not all apps may support this feature.

Split screen view

1   Click the Recents button to open the list of recently used apps.

2   Swipe to the left or right hand side of the screen, click an app's icon, and then click **Open in split screen view**.

3   On the apps list, choose another app to launch.

Launching apps from the Edge panel

1   While using an app, pull the Edge panel handle towards the centre of the screen.

2   Click and hold an app, pull it to the left, and then drop it where **Drop here to open** appears.

The chosen app will launch in the split screen view.

NOTE: You can set to launch an app in the split screen view by clicking it once. click ☰ → **Edit** → ⋮ and click **Tap** under **Open in split screen view**. If you tap the **Show recent apps** switch to activate it, you are able to open the recently used apps in the split screen view from the Edge panel.

Adding app pairs

Add two frequently used apps to the Edge panel to open them together in the split screen view with just one click.

1   In the split screen view, click the circles between the app windows.

2   Tap 🖽.

The two apps you are using in the split screen view are going to be saved on the Edge panel as an app pair.

Adjusting the window size

Pull the circles between the app windows up or down to adjust the size of the windows. When you pull the circles between the app windows to the top or bottom edge of the screen, the window will be maximized.

Pop-up view

1   Click the Recents button to open the list of recently used apps.

2   Swipe to the left or right, click an app's icon, and then click **Open in pop-up view**.

The app screen will display in the pop-up view.

If you click the Home button while using a pop-up window, the window will be minimized and displayed as an app icon. To use the pop-up window again, click the app icon.

Launching apps from the Edge panel

1   Drag the Edge panel handle towards the centre of the screen.

2   Touch and hold an app, pull it to the left, and then drop it where **Drop here for pop-up view** appears.

The chosen app will open in the pop-up view.

Moving pop-up windows

To move a pop-up window, click the window's toolbar and drag it to a new location.

CHAPTER SIX:

OTHER APPS AND FEATURES OF YOUR DEVICE

Samsung Pay

Introduction

Register cards to Samsung Pay to make online and offline payments easily and safely.

You can get additional information, such as cards that support this feature at www.samsung.com/samsung-pay.

NOTE:

- To make payments with Samsung Pay, you may be required to connect the device to a Wi-Fi or mobile network depending on the region.

- Availability of this feature is dependent on the service provider or model.

- The procedures for the initial setup and card registration may not be the same, depending on the service provider or model.

Setting up Samsung Pay

If you're running this app for the first time or restarting it after performing a data reset, follow the instructions displayed on the screen to complete the initial setup.

1   Open the **Samsung Pay** app.

2   Sign in to your Samsung account, then read and agree to the terms and conditions.

3   Register your fingerprint as well as a PIN to use when making payments.

This PIN is going to be used to verify several actions in Samsung Pay, such as making payments and unlocking the app.

Registering cards

Open the **Samsung Pay** app and follow the on-screen instructions to finish your card registration.

Making payments

1   Click and hold a card image at the bottom of the screen and pull it upwards. You can also open the **Samsung Pay** app, then on the cards list, swipe to the left or right and choose a card to use.

2 Scan your fingerprint or input the payment PIN you set.

3 Touch the back of your device to feel the card reader. Once the card reader is able to recognize the card information, the payment will be processed.

NOTE:

- The processing of payments may be affected by your network connection.

- The verification method for payments may not be the same, depending on the card readers.

Cancelling payments

You can cancel payments by visiting the place where you made the transactions.

On the cards list, swipe to the left or right to pick the card you used. Follow the on-screen instructions to complete the cancellation of your payments.

Samsung Health

Introduction

Samsung Health enables you manage your wellness and fitness. Define fitness goals, monitor your progress, and keep track of your overall wellness and fitness. You can also compare your step count records with other Samsung Health users and see other health tips. Please visit www.samsung.com/samsung-health for more details.

Using Samsung Health

Open the **Samsung Health** app. When you want to run this app for the first time or restart it after performing a data reset, use the on-screen guidelines to complete the setup.

To edit items on the Samsung Health home screen, click **Manage items** at the bottom of the trackers list.

Home cards

Monitor your health and fitness.

Compare your step count records with other Samsung Health users or compete with your friends.

Manage your profile and view your health and fitness history.

View health tips.

NOTE:

- Some features may be absent depending on the region.

- If you're using the steps tracker while travelling by car or train, your step count may affect your vibration.

Samsung Notes

Make notes by typing text from the keyboard or by handwriting or drawing on the screen. You can also insert your best-loved images or voice recordings into your notes.

Creating notes

1 Open the **Samsung Notes** app, click ⓔ, and then create a note.

You can change the input method by clicking

 or ⌨

Enter a title

Insert files

Reading mode

2 After composing the note, click the Back button to save it. If you want to save the note in another file format, touch ⋮ → **Save as file**.

Deleting notes

Touch and hold a note to delete and click **Delete**.

Samsung Members

Samsung Members provides support services to customers, such as device problem diagnosis, and allows users submit questions and error reports. You are also able to share information with others in the Galaxy users' community or view the latest news and tips. **Samsung Members** can assist you in solving any problems you might encounter while using your device.

Samsung Kids

You can restrict children's access to some particular apps, set their usage times, and configure settings to give an exciting and safe environment for children when they use the device.

Open the notification panel, swipe downwards, and then click ☺ (**Samsung Kids**) to activate the feature. The Samsung Kids screen will display. If it's not there, click the plus button ⊕ and move it over to add it. When you're using this feature for the first time or after performing a data reset, follow the on-screen instructions to complete the setup.

On the Samsung Kids screen, choose the app you want to use.

NOTE: Your preset screen lock method or your created PIN will be required when activating the **Parental controls** feature or closing Samsung Kids.

Using parental control features

You can configure the settings for Samsung Kids and check the usage history.

On the Samsung Kids screen, click ⋮ → **Parental controls** and input your unlock code.

Closing Samsung Kids

To close Samsung Kids, click the Back button or click ⋮ → **Close Samsung Kids**, and then input your unlock code.

Galaxy Shop

Visit the Samsung website and view various information related to products.

Open the **Galaxy Shop** app.

Galaxy Wearable

Galaxy Wearable is an app that lets you manage your wearable devices. When you connect your device to the wearable device, you can personalize the wearable device's settings and apps.

Open the **Galaxy Wearable** app.

Click the **Start** button to connect your device to the wearable device. Follow the on-screen instructions to finish the setup. Refer to the user manual of the specific wearable device for more information about how to connect and use it with your device.

Calendar

Manage your schedule by putting upcoming events in your planner.

Creating events

1   Open the **Calendar** app and click 🛑 or double-click a date.

    If the date already has saved events or tasks in it, click the date and click 🛑.

2   Enter event details and click **Save**.

Syncing events with your accounts

1   Open the **Settings** app, click **Accounts and backup** →
    Manage accounts, and then choose the account to sync
    with.

2   Click **Sync account** and click the **Calendar** switch to ac-
    tivate it.

To add accounts to sync with, open the **Calendar** app and
click ☰→ ⚙ → **Manage calendars**. Then click thee plus
button ➕ to add account. Then, choose an account to sync
with and sign in. When you add an account, a blue circle is
displayed next to the account name.

Reminder

Register to-do items as reminders and get notifications according to the condition you set.

NOTE:

- To receive more exact notifications, connect to a Wi-Fi
  or mobile network.

- To use location reminders, you must activate the GPS
  feature. Location reminders may be unavailable depending on the model.

Starting Reminder

Open the **Calendar** app and click $\equiv$ → **Reminder**. The Reminder screen will display and the Reminder app icon (⬤) will be added to the Apps screen.

Creating reminders

1   Open the **Reminder** app.

2   Click **Write a reminder** or ⊕, input the details, and then click **Save**.

Completing reminders

On the reminders menu, click ⬜ or just choose a reminder and click **Complete**.

Restoring reminders

Restore reminders that have been completed.

1   On the reminders menu, click $\equiv$ → **Completed**.

2   Choose a category and click **Edit**.

3   Mark items to restore and click **Restore**.
    Reminders will be included in the reminders list and you will be reminded again.

Deleting reminders

To delete a reminder, choose a reminder and click **Delete**. To delete multiple reminders, click and hold a reminder, Mark reminders to delete, and then click **Delete**.

Voice Recorder

Record or play voice recordings.

1 Launch the **Voice Recorder** app.

2 Click ⦿ to start recording. Speak into the microphone.

- Click (**II**) to pause recording.

  - While making a voice recording, click **BOOKMARK** to insert a bookmark.

3 Click ◼ to finish recording.

4 Type a file name and click **Save**.

Changing the recording mode

Choose a mode from the top of the voice recorder screen.

- **Standard**: This is the normal recording mode.

- **Speech-to-text**: The device records your voice and instantly converts it to on-screen text. For best results, place the device close to your mouth and speak loudly and clearly in a place that is quiet.

NOTE: If the voice memo system language does not match the language you are speaking, the device will not recognize your voice. Before you use this feature, click the current language to set the voice memo system language.

My Files

Access and manage different files stored in the device.

Open the **My Files** app.

To search for unnecessary data and free up your device's storage, click **Analyze storage**. To search for files or folders, click Q.

Clock

Set alarms, check the current time in several cities around the world, time an event, or set a particular duration. Open the **Clock** app.

Calculator

Execute simple or complex calculations.

Open the **Calculator** app.

- ⏱ : View the calculation history. To clear the history, click **Clear history**. To close the calculation history panel, click 🖩.

- 📏 : Use the unit conversion tool. You can convert different values, such as area, length, or temperature, into other units.

- ⌨ : Display the scientific calculator.

Game Launcher

Game Launcher collects your games downloaded from **Play Store** and **Galaxy Store** into one place for seamless access. You are able to set the device to game mode to play games more easily.

Open the **Game Launcher** app and choose the game you want.

NOTE:

- If **Game Launcher** does not show, launch the **Settings** app, click **Advanced features**, and then click the **Game Launcher** switch to activate it.

- Games downloaded from **Play Store** and **Galaxy Store** automatically show on the Game Launcher screen. If you cannot see your games, pull the Library panel upwards and click ⋮ → **Add apps**.

Removing a game from Game Launcher

Pull the Library panel upwards, then touch and hold a game, and then click **Remove from Game Launcher**.

Changing the performance mode

You can change the game performance mode.

117

Open the **Game Launcher** app, tap ☰ → **Game perfor-mance** → **Game performance**, and then choose the mode you want.

- **Performance**: This focuses on providing you with the best possible performance while playing games.

- **Standard**: This helps to balance the performance and the battery usage time.

- **Battery saver**: This will help you save battery power while playing games.

NOTE: Efficiency of battery power may vary depending on the game.

Game Booster

Game Booster allows you to play games in a better environ-ment. You can use Game Booster while playing games.

To open the Game Booster panel while playing games, click on the navigation bar. If the navigation bar does not show, drag upwards from the bottom of the screen to show it. If the navigation bar is set to use **Swipe gestures**, open the notification panel and click **Tap to open Game Booster.**

- ⚙ : Configure settings for Game Booster.

- **Priority mode**: Set the device to block incoming calls and all notifications except for alarms so as to prevent any disturbance when playing your game.

- **Monitoring temperature / Monitoring memory**: Configure the device to automatically adjust settings to prevent overheating and to stop apps running in the background to better manage your device's memory.

- **Navigation button lock**: Hide the buttons on the navigation bar away from view. To display the buttons, click 🔒 on the navigation bar.

- **Screen touch lock**: Lock the touchscreen while playing game. To unlock the touchscreen, simply drag the lock icon in any direction.

- **Screenshot**: Capture screenshots.

NOTE:

- You can set to open the Game Booster panel from the navigation bar when the navigation bar is set to **Swipe gestures**. On the Game Booster panel, click ⚙ → **Block during game** and click the **Navigation gestures** switch to activate the feature.

- The options available may vary depending on the game.

Launching apps in pop-up windows while playing games

You can launch apps in pop-up windows even while playing a game.

Click 🎮 and select an app from the apps list.

SmartThings

Take charge of and manage smart appliances and Internet of Things (IoT) products with your smartphone.

To find more information, launch the **SmartThings** app and click ☰ → **How to use**.

1   Launch the **SmartThings** app.

2   Tap **Devices** → **+** or tap **Add device**

3   Choose a device and connect to it by following the on-screen instructions.

NOTE:

- Connection methods may vary according to the type of connected devices or the shared content.

- The devices you can connect vary by region. Available features may not be the same, depending on the connected device.

- Connected devices' own errors or defects are not included in the Samsung warranty. If there are errors or defects on the connected devices, contact the device's manufacturer.

Sharing content

Share content by using different sharing options. The underlisted actions are an example of sharing images.

1 Launch the **Gallery** app and choose an image.

2 Tap ⌗ and choose a sharing method you want.

NOTE: You may be charged extra when sharing files via the mobile network.

Quick Share

Sharing content with nearby devices

Share content with nearby devices using Wi-Fi Direct or Bluetooth, or with SmartThings supported devices.

1   Launch the **Gallery** app and choose an image.

2   On the other device, open the notification panel, swipe downwards, and then click ⊚ (**Quick Share**) to activate the feature. If you don't find it there, click the plus button and move it over to add it.

3   Tap ⌗ → **Quick Share** and choose a device to transfer the image to.

4   Accept the request to transfer file on the other device.

NOTE: This feature is not supported when sharing videos with TVs or SmartThings supported devices. If you like watching videos on TV, then use the Smart View feature.

Setting who can find your device

Determine who is allowed to find and send content to your device.

1   Open the notification panel, swipe downwards, and then click ⊙ (**Quick Share**) to activate the feature.

2   Touch and hold ⊙ (**Quick Share**).

The Quick Share settings screen will display.

3   Choose an option.

   • **Non one**: Don't allow other people to find your device.

   • **Contacts only**: Allow only those in your contacts to share with your device.

   • **Anyone nearby**: Allow any neighboring devices to share with your device.

Link Sharing

Share large files by uploading files to the Samsung storage server and sharing them with others via a Web link.

1   Launch the **Gallery** app and choose an image.

2   Tap ⟨⟨ → **Link Sharing**.

The link for the image will be generated.

3   Choose a sharing option.

Music Share

Introduction

The Music Share feature offers you the liberty to share your Bluetooth speaker that is already connected to your device with another person. You can also listen to the same music on your Galaxy Buds and someone else's Galaxy Buds.

You can get this feature only on devices that support the Music Share feature.

Sharing a Bluetooth speaker

You will be able to listen to music on your smartphone and your friend's smartphone via your Bluetooth speaker.

1 Ensure that your smartphone and your Bluetooth speaker are connected.

Refer to Pairing with other Bluetooth devices to learn more about how to connect.

2   On your smartphone, open the notification panel and swipe down, then check if 🅒 (**Music Share**) has been activated.

You can explore more features, such as setting who to share your device with, by tapping and holding 📱 (**Music Share**).

3   On your friend's smartphone, choose your speaker from the list of the Bluetooth devices.

4   On your smartphone, accept the request for connection. When you do that, your speaker will be shared.

When you play music via your friend's smartphone, the music playing via your smartphone will automatically be paused.

Listening to music together with Galaxy Buds

You can listen to music on your smartphone together via your Buds and your friend's Buds.

This feature is not supported on other models than Galaxy Buds, Galaxy Buds Plus, and Galaxy Buds Live.

1   Make sure that you have connected each smartphone and pair of Buds.

Refer to Pairing with other Bluetooth devices to learn more about how to connect.

2   On the other smartphone, open the notification panel, swipe downwards, and then click (**Music Share**) to activate it.

You can use more features, for example, setting who you share your device with, by tapping and holding (**Music Share**).

3   On your smartphone, open the notification panel and click **Media**.

4   Tap ♪ and choose your friend's Buds from the detected devices list.

5   On your friend's smartphone, accept the request to connect.

6   On your smartphone, mark your Buds and your friend's Buds on the audio output list.

When you play music via your smartphone, both of you can listen to it together through your buds and your friend's.

Smart View

View the content displayed on your device on a large screen by connecting your device to a screen mirroring-enabled TV or monitor.

1 Open the notification panel and swipe down, then click ⊚ (**Smart View**).

2 Choose a device to mirror your device's screen or display content.

NOTE: When you play a video with Smart View, the resolution may change depending on the TV model.

Link to Windows

You can connect your device to a Windows PC to quickly access your device's data, such as pictures or messages, on the computer.

When you have incoming calls or messages, you can receive them on the computer.

NOTE:

· This feature can only be found on Windows 10 version 1803 or higher, and it is recommended to use the latest version to optimize this feature.

· You need to have a Microsoft account in order to use this feature. When you create a Microsoft account, you can sign in to access all Microsoft devices and services, such as Microsoft Office programs and Windows 10.

Connecting to a computer

1 Open the **Settings** app and click **Advanced features** → **Link to Windows**.

2 Follow the on-screen instructions to finish the connection.

To view data and notifications from your smartphone on the computer

Open the **Your Phone** app on the computer and Choose a category you want.

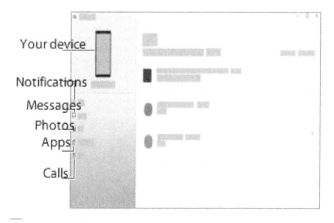

NOTE: Available features and menus may differ depending on the software version or model.

Samsung Global Goals

The Global Goals, which were established by the United Nations General Assembly in 2015, are made up of goals that aim to create a sustainable society. These goals have the influence to eradicate poverty, fight inequality, and stop climate change.

With Samsung Global Goals, learn more about the global goals and join the crusade for a better and healthier future.

Google apps

Google offers entertainment, social network, and business apps. You may need to have a Google account to access some apps.

To view more information about each app and access its help menu:

- **Chrome**: Search for information and browse webpages.

- **Gmail**: Sending or receiving emails via the Google Mail service.

- **Maps**: Find your exact location on the map, search the world map, and view information about you location and different places around you.

- **YT Music**: Enjoy yourself with different music and videos from YouTube Music. You can also view the music collections saved on your device and play them.

- **Play Movies & TV**: Purchase or rent videos, e.g. movies and TV programmes, from **Play Store**.

- **Drive**: Store your content on the cloud, access it from anywhere and anytime, and share it with others.

- **YouTube**: Watch or create your own videos and share them with others.

- **Photos**: Search for, manage, and edit all your pictures and videos from different sources in one location.

- **Google**: Browse items on the Internet or your device.

- **Duo**: Make a simple video call.

- **Messages**: Send and receive messages on your device or computer, and share different types of content, e.g. images and videos.

NOTE: You may not find some apps, depending on the service provider or model.

CHAPTER SEVEN: SETTINGS

Introduction

Learn how to customization of your device settings.

Launch the **Settings** app.

To search for settings by entering keywords, click Q.

Samsung account

Sign in to your Samsung account and manage it as desired.

On the Settings screen, click **Samsung account**.

Connections

Options

Change settings for different connections, like the Wi-Fi feature and Bluetooth.

On the Settings screen, click **Connections**.

- **Wi-Fi**: Activate the Wi-Fi feature to enable you connect to a Wi-Fi network and access the Internet or other network devices. Refer to Wi-Fi for additional information.

- **Bluetooth**: Use Bluetooth to transfer and/or receive data or media files with other Bluetooth-enabled devices. Refer to Bluetooth for additional information.

- **NFC and contactless payments**: Set the device to let you read near field communication (NFC) tags that have information about products. You can also use this feature to make transactions and buy tickets for transportation or events after downloading the needed apps. Refer to NFC and contactless payments for further details.

- **Flight mode**: Make your device to disable all wireless functions on it. You'll only be able to use non-network services.

  CAUTION: Follow the guidelines provided by the airline and the relevant instructions of aircraft personnel. In some circumstances where it is permitted to use the device, always use it in flight mode.

- **Mobile networks**: Configure the settings of your mobile network.

- **Data usage**: Keep up with your data usage amount and customize the settings for the limitation. Set the device to automatically disable the mobile data connection when the amount of mobile data you have used reaches the limit you have specified.

  You can activate the data saver feature to prevent some apps running in the background from sending or receiving data so as to minimize data usage. Refer to Data saver for further information.

You can also choose apps that should always use the mobile data even when your device is connected to a Wi-Fi network. Refer to Mobile data only apps for further details.

- **SIM card manager** (dual SIM models): Activate your SIM or USIM cards and also customize the SIM card settings. Refer to SIM card manager (dual SIM models) for additional information.

- **Mobile Hotspot and Tethering**: Use the device as a mobile hotspot to share the its own mobile data connection with other devices. For more information about this feature, refer to Mobile Hotspot.

NOTE: You may incur extra charges when using this feature.

- **More connection settings**: You can customize settings to allow you control other features. Refer to More connection settings for more information.

Wi-Fi

Activate the Wi-Fi feature to connect your device to a Wi-Fi network and be able to access the Internet or other network devices.

Connecting to a Wi-Fi network

1 On the Settings screen, click **Connections** → **Wi-Fi** and touch the switch to activate the feature.

2 Choose a network from the Wi-Fi networks list.

Networks with a lock icon means you need a password to connect to them.

NOTE:

• After the device has successfully connected to a Wi-Fi network for the first time, the device will reconnect to that network any other time it is available without requiring a password. To prevent the device from connecting to the network automatically, click ⚙ next to the network and click the **Auto reconnect** switch to deactivate it.

• If you're finding difficulty connecting to a Wi-Fi network properly, restart your device's Wi-Fi feature or the wireless router.

Viewing the Wi-Fi network quality information

View the Wi-Fi network quality information, e.g. the speed and stability.

On the Settings screen, click **Connections** → **Wi-Fi** and click the switch to activate it. The network quality information will display under the Wi-Fi networks. If it does not display, click ⋮ → **Advanced** and click the **Show network quality info** switch to activate it.

NOTE: The quality information may not show depending on the Wi-Fi network.

Sharing Wi-Fi network passwords

If you make a request to someone who is connected to a secured Wi-Fi network to share its password, you can connect to the network without entering the password. This feature is available between the devices which have contacts with each other and the you must ensure the screen of the other device is turned on.

1 On the Settings screen, click **Connections** → **Wi-Fi** and click the switch to activate it.

2 Choose a network from the Wi-Fi networks list.

3 Click **Request password**.

4 Accept the share request on the other device.

   The Wi-Fi password is automatically entered on your device and will be connected to the network.

Wi-Fi Direct

Wi-Fi Direct connects devices directly via a Wi-Fi network without needing an access point.

1   On the Settings screen, click **Connections** → **Wi-Fi** and click the switch to activate it.

2   Click ⦂ → **Wi-Fi Direct**.

   The list of detected devices is displayed.

If the device you want to connect to is not shown on the list, request that the device turns on its Wi-Fi Direct feature.

3   Choose a device to connect to.

The devices will be connected when the other device accepts the request for Wi-Fi Direct connection.

To terminate the device connection, select the device to disconnect from the list.

Bluetooth

Use Bluetooth for exchange of data or media files with other Bluetooth-enabled devices.

CAUTION:

- Samsung is not accountable for the loss, interception, or misuse of data sent or received via Bluetooth.
- Always make sure that you share and receive data with devices that are trusted and properly secured. If there are impediments between the devices, the operating distance may be reduced.
- Some devices may not be compatible with your device, especially those that are not tested or approved by the Bluetooth SIG.
- Never use the Bluetooth feature for illegal purposes (for example, pirating copies of files or illegally tapping

communications for commercial purposes). Samsung will not take responsibility for the repercussion of illegal use of the Bluetooth feature.

Pairing with other Bluetooth devices

1   On the Settings screen, click **Connections** → **Bluetooth** and click the switch to activate it. A list of the detected devices will pop up.

2   Choose a device to pair with.

    If the device you want to pair with is not displayed on the list, then set the device to enter Bluetooth pairing mode. Refer to the other user manual of the other device.

NOTE: Your device will be visible to other devices while the Bluetooth settings screen is open.

3   Accept the Bluetooth connection request on your device to establish the connection.

    The devices become connected when the other device accepts the Bluetooth connection request.

    To unpair the devices, click ⚙ next to the device name and click **Unpair**.

Sending and receiving data

Several apps support data transfer via Bluetooth. You are able to share data, such as contacts or media files, with other

Bluetooth devices. The underlisted actions are an example of sending an image to another device.

1   Open the **Gallery** app and choose an image.

2   Tap ⊲ᵒ → **Bluetooth** and choose a device to transfer the image to.

If the device you want to pair with is not in the list, request the device to turn on its visibility option.

3   Accept the request for Bluetooth connection on the other device.

NFC and contactless payments

Your device lets you read near field communication (NFC) tags that have information about products. You can also use this feature to make business transactions and purchase tickets for transportation or events after you have downloaded the relevant apps.

CAUTION: Your device contains a built-in NFC antenna. Handle the device with care to avoid damaging the NFC antenna.

Reading information from NFC tags

Make use of the NFC feature to read product information from NFC tags.

1 On the Settings screen, click **Connections** and click the **NFC and contactless payments** switch to activate it.

2 Place the NFC antenna area on the back of your device close to an NFC tag. The information from the tag will display.

NOTE: Make sure the device's screen is turned on and un-locked. If not, the device will not read NFC tags or re-ceive data.

Making payments with the NFC feature

Before you can use the NFC feature to make payments, you must first of all register for the mobile payment service. If you want to register or get more information about the ser-vice, contact your service provider.

1   On the Settings screen, click **Connections** and click the **NFC and contactless payments** switch to activate the feature.

2   Use the NFC antenna area on the back of your device to touch the NFC card reader.

To set the default payment app, open the Settings screen and click **Connections → NFC and contactless payments → Contactless payments → Payment**, and then choose an app.

NOTE: All available payment apps may not be included in the payment services list.

Data saver

Minimize your data usage by preventing some apps running in the background from sending or receiving data.

On the Settings screen, click **Connections → Data usage → Data saver** and click the switch to activate it.

When the data saver feature is activated, the icon will display on the status bar.

Data saver feature activated

  To select apps to use data without restriction, click **Allowed to use data while Data saver is on** and select apps.

Mobile data only apps

Choose apps to always use the mobile data even when your device is connected to a Wi-Fi network.

For instance, you can set the device to use only mobile data for apps that you want to keep secure or streaming apps that can be disconnected. Even though you do not deactivate the Wi-Fi feature, the apps will start using the mobile data.

On the Settings screen, click **Connections** → **Data usage** → **Mobile data only apps**, tap the switch to activate it, and then tap the other switches next to the apps you want.

NOTE: You may incur extra charges when using this feature.

Mobile Hotspot

To use your device as a mobile hotspot to share your device's mobile data connection with other devices, follow these steps:

1 On the Settings screen, click **Connections** → **Mobile Hotspot and Tethering** → **Mobile Hotspot**.

2 Click the switch to activate it.

   The 🛜 icon will show on the status bar.

   You can reconfigure the level of security and the password by tapping **Configure**.

3 On the other device's screen, search for your device from the Wi-Fi networks list and select it. Alternatively, click

QR code on the mobile hotspot screen and scan the QR code with the other device.

NOTE:

- If you can't find the mobile hotspot on your device, click **Configure** and set **Band** to 2.4 GHz, click **Advanced**, and then click the **Hidden network** switch to deactivate it.

- When you activate the **Auto Hotspot** feature, you can share your device's mobile data connection with other devices signed in to your Samsung account.

More connection settings

Personalize settings to control other connection features.

From the Settings screen, click **Connections** → **More connection settings**.

- **Nearby device scanning**: Make the device to scan for nearby devices to connect to.

- **Printing**: Configure settings for printer plug-ins installed on your smartphone. You can search for available printers or add them manually to print files. Refer to Printing for further information.

- **VPN**: Set up virtual private networks (VPNs) on your smartphone to connect to a school or company's private network.

- **Private DNS**: Set your smartphone to use the security enhanced private DNS.

- **Ethernet**: As soon as you connect an Ethernet adaptor, you can use a wired network and configure network settings.

Printing

Configure settings for printer plug-ins installed on your smartphone. You can connect your smartphone to a printer via Wi-Fi or Wi-Fi Direct, and print images or documents.

NOTE: Some printers may not be compatible with your smartphone.

Adding printer plug-ins

Add printer plug-ins for the printers that you want to connect your device to.

1   From the Settings screen, click **Connections** → **More connection settings** → **Printing** → **Download plugin**.

2   Choose a printer plug-in and install it.

3   Choose the installed printer plug-in.

Your smartphone will automatically search for printers that are connected to the same Wi-Fi network as itself.

4 Pick a printer to add.

NOTE: To add printers manually, click ⋮ → **Add printer**.

Printing content

While viewing content, such as images or documents, access the options list, click **Print** → ▼ → **All printers...**, and then choose a printer.

NOTE: Printing methods may differ depending on the content type.

Sounds and vibration

Options

Change settings for different sounds on the device.

On the Settings screen, click **Sounds and vibration**.

- **Sound mode**: Make the device to use sound mode, vibration mode, or silent mode.

- **Vibrate while ringing**: Make the device to vibrate and play a ringtone for incoming calls.

- **Temporary mute**: Make the device to use silent mode for a certain period.

- **Ringtone**: Change the call ringtone.

- **Notification sound**: Change the notification sound.

- **System sound**: Alter the sound to use for some kinds of actions, such as charging the device.

- **Volume**: Regulate the device's volume level.

- **Call vibration pattern**: Change the call vibration pattern.

- **Notification vibration pattern**: Change the notification vibration pattern.

- **Vibration intensity**: Regulate the force of the vibration notification.

- **System sound/vibration control**: Make the device to sound or vibrate for actions, such as controlling the touchscreen.

- **Sound quality and effects**: Set the sound quality and effects of the device. Refer to Sound quality and effects for further information.

- **Separate app sound**: Make the device to play media sound from a specific app separately on the other audio device. Refer to Separate app sound for further information.

NOTE: Some features may be unavailable depending on the model.

Sound quality and effects

Set the device's sound quality and effects.

On the Settings screen, click **Sounds and vibration** → **Sound quality and effects**.

- **Dolby Atmos**: Choose a surround sound mode optimized for different types of audio, such as movies, music, and voice. Using Dolby Atmos, you can experience moving audio sounds that flow all around you.

- **Dolby Atmos for gaming**: Experience the Dolby Atmos sound optimized for games as you play games.

- **Equalizer**: Choose an option for a specific music genre and enjoy optimized sound.

- **UHQ upscaler**: Increase the sound resolution of music and videos.

- **Adapt sound**: Make the best sound for you.

NOTE: Subject to the model, you must connect an earphone to use some features.

Separate app sound

Make the device to play media sound from a specific app on the connected Bluetooth speaker or headset.

For example, you can listen to the Navigation app through your device's speaker while at the same time listening to playback from the Music app through the vehicle's Bluetooth speaker.

1   On the Settings screen, click **Sounds and vibration** → **Separate app sound** and click the switch to activate it.

2   Choose an app to play media sounds separately and click the Back button.

3   Choose a device for playing the chosen app's media sound.

Notifications

Change the notification settings.

On the Settings screen, click **Notifications**.

- **Notification pop-up style**: Choose a notification pop-up style and change the settings.

- **Recently sent**: See the apps that received recent notifications and change the notification settings. To personalize notification settings for more apps, click **More** → ▼ → **All** and choose an app from the apps list.

- **Do not disturb**: Configure your smartphone to mute all sounds apart from the allowed exceptions.

- **Advanced settings**: Configure advanced settings for notifications.

Display

Options

Change the display and the Home screen settings.

On the Settings screen, click **Display**.

- **Light / Dark**: Activate or deactivate the dark mode feature.

- **Dark mode settings**: Reduce strain on your eye by applying the dark theme whenever you're using the device at night or in a dark place. You can set a schedule for when to apply dark mode.

NOTE:

The dark theme may not work in some apps.

- **Brightness**: Regulate the brightness of the display.

- **Adaptive brightness**: Make the device to keep up to date with your brightness adjustments and apply them automatically in similar lighting conditions.

- **Motion smoothness**: Modify the refresh rate of the screen. When you set high refresh rate, the screen will scroll more smoothly and seamlessly. Refer to Motion smoothness for further information.

- **Eye comfort shield**: Reduce eye strain by reducing the amount of blue light that is emitted by the screen. You can set a plan for applying this feature.

- **Screen mode**: Change the screen mode to regulate the display's colour and contrast. Refer to Changing the screen mode or adjusting the display colour for further information.

- **Font size and style**: Modify the font size and style.

- **Screen zoom**: Make the items on the screen bigger or smaller.

- **Full screen apps**: Choose apps to use with the full screen aspect ratio.

- **Screen timeout**: Set how long the device waits before turning off the display's backlight.

- **Easy mode**: Switch to easy mode to show larger icons and apply a simpler layout to the Home screen.

- **Edge panels**: Modify the settings for the Edge panel.

- **Navigation bar**: Change the navigation bar settings. Refer to Navigation bar (soft buttons) for further information.

- **Accidental touch protection**: Make the device's screen not detect any touch input when it is in a dark place, such as a pocket or bag.

- **Touch sensitivity**: Increase the touch sensitivity of the screen when used with screen protectors.

- **Show charging information**: Set the device to show the charging information, such as the remaining battery percentage when the screen is off.

- **Screen saver**: Set the device to start a screen saver when the device is charging.

NOTE: Some features may not be found depending on the model.

Motion smoothness

The refresh rate refers to the number of times the screen is refreshed every second. Use a high refresh rate so that the screen does not glimmer when switching between screens. The screen will scroll more smoothly. Your battery usage will reduce when you select a standard refresh rate, meaning you can use the battery longer.

1   On the Settings screen, click **Display** → **Motion smoothness**.

2   Choose a refresh rate.

- **High**: Experience a smooth animations and scrolling by automatically regulating your screen refresh rate up to 90 Hz (SM-A525F, SM-A725F) / 120 Hz (SM-A526B).

- **Standard**: Use a standard refresh rate in normal situations to reduce battery power consumption.

To Change the screen mode or adjust the display colour:

Change the screen mode or adjust the display colour to your favourite.

Changing the screen mode

On the Settings screen, click **Display** → **Screen mode** and choose a mode you want.

- **Vivid**: This enhances the colour range, saturation, as well as the sharpness of your display. You can also alter the display colour balance by colour value.
- **Natural**: This alters the screen to a natural tone.

   NOTE: You cannot adjust the display colour except in **Vivid** mode.

- **Vivid** mode may function well with third-party apps.

Optimizing the full screen colour balance

improve the display colour by adjusting the colour tones to your own preference. On the Settings screen, click **Display** → **Screen mode** → **Vivid** and fine-tune the colour adjustment bar under **White balance**.

When you pull the colour adjustment bar towards **Cool**, the blue colour tone will increase. When you pull the bar towards **Warm**, the red colour tone will increase.

Adjusting the screen tone by colour value

Increase or lower certain colour tones by modifying the Red, Green, or Blue value individually.

1   On the Settings screen, click **Display** → **Screen mode** → **Vivid**.

2   Tap **Advanced settings**.

3   Adjust the **R** (Red), **G** (Green), or **B** (Blue) colour bar as desired. The screen tone will be adjusted.

Wallpaper

Modify the wallpaper settings for the Home screen and the locked screen. On the Settings screen, click **Wallpaper**.

Themes

Apply different themes to your smartphone to change the visual elements of the Home screen, locked screen, and icons. On the Settings screen, click **Themes**.

CHAPTER EIGHT:
SETTINGS (PART 2)

Home screen

Configure your personal settings for the Home screen, such as the screen layout.

On the Settings screen, click **Home screen**.

Lock screen

Options

Modify the settings for the locked screen.

On the Settings screen, click **Lock screen**.

- **Screen lock type**: Modify the screen lock method.

- **Smart Lock**: Make the device to unlock itself when trusted locations or devices are detected. Refer to Smart Lock for further information.

- **Secure lock settings**: Modify screen lock settings for the chosen lock method.

- **Always On Display**: Set the device to display information while the screen is turned off. See Always On Display for more information.

- **Wallpaper services**: Make the device to utilize wallpaper services such as Dynamic Lock screen.

- **Clock style**: Modify the type and colour of the clock on the locked screen.

- **Roaming clock**: Alternate the clock to show both the local and home time zones on the locked screen when roaming.

- **Widgets**: Change the settings of the items that are displayed on the locked screen.

- **Contact information**: Make the device to show contact information, such as your email address, on the locked screen.

- **Notifications**: Set how notifications should show on the locked screen.

- **Shortcuts**: Choose apps to display shortcuts to them on the locked screen.

- **About Lock screen**: Take a look at the Lock screen version and legal information.

NOTE: The available options may be different depending on the screen lock method you have chosen.

Smart Lock

You can configure the smartphone to unlock itself and stay unlocked when trusted locations or devices are detected.

For example, if you have set your home or office as a trusted location, whenever you get home or to your office, your device will detect the location and automatically unlock itself. On the Settings screen, click **Lock screen** → **Smart Lock** and follow the on-screen instructions to finish the setup.

NOTE:

- You will be able to use this feature only after you have set a screen lock method.
- If you have not used your device for at least four hours or when you turn it on, you must have to unlock the screen by using the pattern, PIN, or password you set.

Always On Display

You can view some information, such as the clock or calendar, or control music playback on the screen when it is turned off.

You can also find out about notifications for new messages or missed calls.

The Always On Display is set to appear only when you tap the screen. To change the settings to make it display non-stop or during a set time, on the Settings screen, click **Lock screen** → **Always On Display**, and then choose a mode you want.

NOTE: The brightness of the Always On Display may change any time automatically based on the lighting conditions.

Opening notifications on the Always On Display

When you receive message, missed call, or app notifications, notification icons will show on the Always On Display. Double-click a notification icon to view its notification.

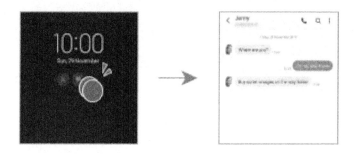

NOTE: If the screen is locked, you must first of all unlock it to view notifications.

Deactivating the Always On Display feature

Open the notification panel, swipe down, and then click ⊡ (**Always On Display**) to deactivate it. If you don't find it on the quick panel, click on the plus button and move it over to add it.

Alternatively, on the Settings screen, click **Lock screen**, and then click the **Always On Display** switch to deactivate it.

Biometrics and security

Options

Modify the settings for securing your device.

On the Settings screen, click **Biometrics and security**.

- **Face recognition**: Set your smartphone to unlock the screen by recognizing your face. Refer to *Face recognition* for detailed information.

- **Fingerprints**: Register your fingerprints for you to unlock the screen. Refer to *Fingerprint recognition* for additional information.

- **More biometrics settings**: Modify the settings for biometric data. You can also view the version of the biometrics security patch and check for updates.

- **Google Play Protect**: Make the device to check for harmful apps and behaviour and warn about potential harm and remove them.

- **Security update**: Ascertain the version of your device's software and check for updates.

- **Find My Mobile**: Activate or deactivate the feature for Find My Mobile. Access the Find My Mobile website (findmymobile.samsung.com) to track and control your device if it gets lost or stolen.

- **Samsung Pass**: Verify your identity easily and safely through your biometric data. Refer to *Samsung Pass* for additional information.

- **Secure Folder**: Create a secure folder to help you protect your private content and apps from others. See *Secure Folder* for more information.

- **Secure Wi-Fi**: Configure the device to protect your data anytime you're using unsecured Wi-Fi networks.

- **Private Share**: Share files with others through a secure means using blockchain technology.

- **Samsung Blockchain Keystore**: Manage your blockchain private key safely.

- **Install unknown apps**: Set your device to allow the installation of apps from unknown sources.

- **Encrypt SD card**: Set your device to encrypt files on a memory card.

CAUTION:

If you have this setting enabled in your device when you reset your device to the factory defaults, the device will not be able to read your encrypted files. You must first of all disable this setting before resetting the device.

- **Other security settings**: Configure additional security settings.

NOTE: You may not find some features available depending on the service provider or model.

Face recognition

You can set the device to unlock the screen by merely recognizing your face.

NOTE:

· If you use your face as a screen lock method, your face cannot be used to unlock the screen for the first time you turn on the device. To use the device, you must first of all unlock the screen using the pattern, PIN, or password that you set when registering the face. Be cautious not to forget your pattern, PIN, or password.

· If you change the screen lock method to **Swipe** or **None**, which are not safe methods, all of your biometric data will be removed. If you choose to use your biometric data in apps or features, you must re-register your biometric data.

Precautions for using face recognition

Before using the face recognition to unlock your device, remember the following precautions:

• Someone or something else that looks like your image could be able to unlock your device.

- Face recognition is not as secure as Pattern, PIN, or Password.

For better face recognition

Consider the following when using face recognition:

- Consider the circumstances under which you're registering, such as wearing glasses, hats, masks, beards, or heavy makeup
- Make sure you're in a well-lit area and that the camera lens is clean when registering
- Be sure your image is not blurry for better match results

Registering your face

For a more accurate face registration, register your face indoors and avoid direct sunlight.

1 From the Settings screen, click **Biometrics and security** → **Face recognition**.

2 Read the on-screen instructions and click **Continue**.

3 Set a screen lock method.

4 Select whether you are wearing glasses or not and click **Continue**.

5 Position your face inside the frame on the screen to enable the camera to scan your face.

NOTE:

- If unlocking the screen with your face is not working appropriately, click **Remove face data** to remove your registered face and register your face again.
- To improve the face recognition, click **Add alternative look** and add an alternate appearance.

Unlocking the screen with your face

You can use your face to unlock the device's screen instead of using a pattern, PIN, or password.

1 On the Settings screen, click **Biometrics and security** → **Face recognition**.

2 Unlock the screen by simply using the preset screen lock method.

3 Click the **Face unlock** switch to activate the feature.

4 On the locked screen, look directly at the screen.

If it recognizes your face, you can unlock the screen without using any extra screen lock method. If your face is not recognized, then you have to use the preset screen lock method.

Deleting the registered face data

You can remove face data that you have registered.

1 On the Settings screen, click **Biometrics and security** → **Face recognition**.

2 Unlock the screen by using the preset screen lock method.

3 Click **Remove face data** → **Remove**.

As soon as the registered face is deleted, all the related features will also be deactivated.

Fingerprint recognition

In order for fingerprint recognition to function, you have to first of all register and store your fingerprint information in your device.

NOTE:

- Availability of this feature depends on the service provider or model.

- Fingerprint recognition uses the unique characteristics of each fingerprint to increase the security of your device. The likelihood of the fingerprint sensor confusing two different fingerprints is very minimal. Nevertheless, in rare occasions where separate fingerprints are very similar, the sensor may recognize them as alike.

- If you use a screen protector, ensure it permits for use of the On-screen fingerprint sensor.

- If you use your fingerprint as a screen lock method, you will not be able to use it to unlock the screen for the first time after turning on the device. To use the device, you must first of all unlock the screen using the pattern, PIN, or password you set during the registration of the fingerprint. Be cautious not to forget your pattern, PIN, or password.

- If the device does not recognize your fingerprint, unlock the device using the pattern, PIN, or password you set during the registration of the fingerprint, and then register your fingerprints again. If you forget your pattern, PIN, or password, you will not be able to use the device unless you reset it. Samsung is not accountable for any loss of data or inconvenience that may be caused by forgotten unlock codes.

- If you change the screen lock method to **Swipe** or **None**, which do no give adequate security, all of your biometric data will be deleted from the device. If you want to use your biometric data in apps or features, you must first re-register your biometric data.

For better fingerprint recognition

When you scan your fingerprints on the device, be conscious of the following conditions that may affect the feature's performance:

- The device may not be able to recognize fingerprints if they are affected by wrinkles or scars.
- The device may not recognize fingerprints from fingers that are too small or thin.

- In order to improve recognition performance, register fingerprints of the hand that is most often used to operate the device.

- There is a built-in fingerprint recognition sensor at the bottom centre of your device's screen. Make sure that you secure the screen protector or the touchscreen on the fingerprint recognition sensor area from scratches or damages by objects, such as coins, keys, pens, and necklaces.

- Make sure that the fingerprint recognition sensor area right at the bottom centre of the screen and your fingers are clean and dry when fingerprinting.

- If your finger is not placed properly on the surface of the fingerprint recognition area, the device may not recognize your fingerprints. Avoid bending your finger or using a fingertip. Press the screen tightly with your finger in a way that your fingertip spreads over the wide surface of the fingerprint recognition area.

Registering fingerprints

1 On the Settings screen, click **Biometrics and security** → **Fingerprints**.

2 Read the on-screen instructions and click **Continue**.

3 Set a screen lock method.

4 position your finger on the fingerprint recognition sensor. When the device detects your finger, pull it up and place it on the fingerprint recognition sensor again. Repeat the process until the fingerprint is registered.

5 When you are through registering your fingerprints, click **Done**.

You can check whether your fingerprint is registered by clicking **Check added fingerprints**.

Unlocking the screen with your fingerprints

You can unlock the screen with your fingerprint if you do not want to use a pattern, PIN, or password.

1 On the Settings screen, click **Biometrics and security** → **Fingerprints**.

2 Unlock the screen by using the preset screen lock technique.

3 Click the **Fingerprint unlock** switch to activate it.

4   On the locked screen, put your finger on the fingerprint recognition sensor and scan your fingerprint.

Changing the fingerprint recognition icon setting

Set the device to display or hide the fingerprint recognition icon when you click the screen while the screen is turned off.

1   From the Settings screen, click **Biometrics and security → Fingerprints**.

2   Unlock the screen by using the preset screen lock technique.

3   Click **Show icon when screen is off** and choose an option.

Deleting registered fingerprints

You can delete registered fingerprints.

1   On the Settings screen, click **Biometrics and security → Fingerprints**.

2   Unlock the screen by using the preset screen lock method.

3   Select a fingerprint to delete and click **Remove**.

Samsung Pass

Register your biometric data to Samsung Pass and easily verify your identity when using services which have need of your login or personal information.

NOTE:

- You can use the website sign-in feature only for websites that you access via the **Internet** app. Some websites may not support this feature.

- Registered biometric data is saved to your device alone. It is not synced with other devices or servers.

Registering Samsung Pass

Before using Samsung Pass, you have to register your biometric data to Samsung Pass.

On the Settings screen, click **Biometrics and security** → **Samsung Pass**. Complete the setup by following the on-screen instructions.

Verifying the Samsung account password

You can use your registered biometric data to confirm your identity instead of using your Samsung account password wherever necessary, e.g. when you purchase content from **Galaxy Store**.

On the Samsung Pass main screen, click ⋮ → **Settings** → **Account and syncing**, and then click the **Verify with Samsung Pass** switch to activate it.

Using Samsung Pass to sign in to websites

Samsung Pass can be used to easily sign in to websites that support ID and password autofill.

1   On the sign-in page of the website, input your ID and password, and then click the website's sign-in button.

2   When a pop-up window asking whether you want to save the sign-in information displays, mark **Sign in with Samsung Pass** and click **Remember**.

Using Samsung Pass to sign in to apps

Samsung Pass can be used to easily sign in to apps that support ID and password autofill.

1   On the sign-in page of the app, input your ID and password, and then click the app's sign-in button.

2   When a pop-up window asking whether you want to save the sign-in information displays, click **Save**.

Managing sign-in information

Take a look the list of websites and apps you have set to use Samsung Pass and manage information about your sign-in.

1   On the Samsung Pass main screen, click **Apps** or **Websites** and choose a website or app from the list.

2   Click **Edit** and change your ID, password, and the website's or app's name.

To delete your sign-in information, click **Delete**.

Using Samsung Pass with websites and apps

If you're using websites or apps that support Samsung Pass, you can easily sign in with Samsung Pass.

To know if a website and app supports Samsung Pass, on the Samsung Pass main screen, click ⋮ → **Partners**. If there are no websites or apps that support Samsung Pass, you will not see **Partners**.

NOTE:

- Available websites and apps may differ according to the service provider or model.

- Samsung is not accountable for any loss or inconvenience arising from signing in to websites or apps via Samsung Pass.

Entering your personal information automatically

Your Samsung Pass can be used to easily enter your personal information, such as your address or payment card information, on apps that support autofill.

1 On the Samsung Pass main screen, choose an option under **Private info**.

2 Enter the information and click **Save**.

   You can now use the biometric data you registered to Samsung Pass when entering the personal information automatically on apps that support this feature.

Deleting your Samsung Pass data

You can be able delete your biometric data, sign-in information, and app data registered to Samsung Pass.

From the Samsung Pass main screen, click ⋮ → **Settings** →

See all devices using Samsung Pass → ⋮ → **Leave Samsung Pass**.

NOTE:

- Your Samsung account will remain active.

- The Samsung Pass data on other devices signed in to your Samsung account will also be deleted.

Secure Folder

Secure Folder helps you to secure your private content and apps, such as pictures and contacts, from being accessed by others even when the device is unlocked.

CAUTION:

> Secure Folder is a distinct, secured storage area. You cannot transfer the data in Secure Folder to other devices by means of unauthorized sharing methods, such as USB or Wi-Fi Direct. Any attempt to personalize the operating system or modifying software will cause Secure Folder to be automatically locked and inaccessible. Before saving data in Secure Folder, be sure you have a back up copy of the data in another secure location.

Setting up Secure Folder

1 Start the **Settings** app and click **Biometrics and security** → **Secure Folder**.

2 Complete the setup by following the on-screen instructions.

The Secure Folder screen will display and the Secure Folder app icon (⬛) will be added to the Apps screen. To modify the name or icon colour of Secure Folder, click ⋮ → **Customize**.

NOTE:

• When you start the **Secure Folder** app, you'll have to unlock the app using your preset lock technique.

• If you forget your Secure Folder unlock code, you will not be able to reset it using your Samsung account. Click the button at the bottom of the locked screen, and input your Samsung account password.

Setting an auto lock condition for Secure Folder

1 Start the **Secure Folder** app and click ⋮ → **Settings** → **Auto lock Secure Folder**.

2 Choose a lock option.

NOTE: To manually lock your Secure Folder, click ⋮ → **Lock and exit**.

Moving content to Secure Folder

Transfer content, such as pictures and videos, to Secure Folder. The following procedures are an example of moving an image from the default storage to Secure Folder.

1   Start the **Secure Folder** app and click ⁝ → **Add files**.

2   Click **Images**, tick images to move, and then click **Done**.

3   Click **Move**.

The ticked items will be deleted from the original folder and moved to Secure Folder. To copy items, click **Copy**.

NOTE: The method for moving content may not be the same, depending on the content type.

Adding apps

Add an app to use in Secure Folder.

1   Start the **Secure Folder** app and tap ✛.

2   Choose one or more apps installed on your smartphone and click **Add**.

Removing apps from Secure Folder

Click and hold an app to delete, and click **Uninstall**.

Adding accounts

Add any of your accounts, like Samsung and Google accounts, or other accounts, to sync with the apps in Secure Folder.

1 Launch the **Secure Folder** app and click ⁝ → **Settings** → **Manage accounts** → **Add account**.

2 Choose an account service.

3 Complete the account setup by following the on-screen instructions.

Hiding Secure Folder

You will be able to hide the Secure Folder shortcut, if you like, from the Apps screen.

Launch the **Secure Folder** app, tap ⁝ → **Settings**, and then click the **Show icon on Apps screen** switch to deactivate it.

Alternatively, open the notification panel, swipe down, and then click 🔘 (**Secure Folder**) to deactivate the feature.

If you want the Secure Folder to be visible again, start the **Settings** app, click **Biometrics and security** → **Secure Folder**, and then click the **Show icon on Apps screen** switch to activate it.

Uninstalling Secure Folder

If you wish to, you can uninstall Secure Folder, including the content and apps in it any time.

Start the **Secure Folder** app and click ⁝ → **Settings** → **More settings** → **Uninstall**.

If you want to backup your content before uninstalling Secure Folder, tick **Move media files out of Secure Folder** and click **Uninstall**. To access data you have backed up from Secure Folder, open the **My Files** app and click **Internal storage → Secure Folder**.

NOTE: Notes saved in **Samsung Notes** are not going to have a backup.

Secure Wi-Fi

Secure Wi-Fi is a service that secures your Wi-Fi network connection. It encrypts data by using Wi-Fi networks and also disables tracking apps and websites in a way that you can use Wi-Fi networks securely.

For example, when using an unsecure Wi-Fi network in public places, such as cafes or airports, Secure Wi-Fi is automatically activated in a manner that no one will be able to hack your login information or watch your activity in apps and websites.

From the Settings screen, click **Biometrics and security → Secure Wi-Fi** and follow the on-screen guidelines to complete the setup.

When you activate the Secure Wi-Fi, the 🛡 icon will show on the status bar.

NOTE:

- Using this feature may result in a decreased Wi-Fi network speed.

- This feature may not be available depending on the Wi-Fi network, service provider, or model.

Selecting apps to protect using Secure Wi-Fi

Choose apps to protect using Secure Wi-Fi in order to safely protect data, such as your password or your activity in apps, from being accessed by anyone else.

From the Settings screen, click **Biometrics and security** → **Secure Wi-Fi** → **Protected apps** and click the switches next to the apps you want to protect using Secure Wi-Fi.

NOTE: Some apps may not support this feature.

Purchasing protection plan

You are given a free protection plan for Wi-Fi networks each month. You can as well purchase paid protection plans and get unlimited bandwidth protection for a restricted time.

1   From the Settings screen, click **Biometrics and security** → **Secure Wi-Fi**.

2   Click **Protection plan** and choose the plan you want.

NOTE: For some kind of protection plans, you can transfer the protection plan to another device signed in to your Samsung account.

3   Complete the purchase by following the on-screen instructions.

Privacy

Modify the settings for privacy.

On the Settings screen, click **Privacy**.

- **Permission manager**: Take a look at the list of features and apps that have permission to use them. You can also edit the permission settings.
- **Samsung**: Manage personal data related to your Samsung account and modify the settings for Customization Service.
- **Google**: Configure advanced settings for privacy.

NOTE: Some features may not be available depending upon the service provider or model.

Location

Edit settings for location information permissions.

On the Settings screen, click **Location**.

- **App permissions**: View the list of apps that have permission to access the device's location and change the permission settings.

- **Improve accuracy**: Make the device to use the Wi-Fi or Bluetooth feature to increase the accuracy of your location information, even though the features are deactivated.

- **Recent location requests**: You can see which apps request your present location information.

- **Location services**: View the location services your device is making use of.

Google

Configure settings for some features offered by Google.

On the Settings screen, click **Google**.

Accounts and backup

Options

Sync, back up, or restore your smartphone's data using Samsung Cloud. You can also sign in to accounts, such as your Samsung account or Google account, or transfer data to or from other devices by using Smart Switch.

On the Settings screen, click **Accounts and backup**.

- **Manage accounts**: Add your Samsung and Google accounts, or other accounts, to sync with.

- **Samsung Cloud**: Back up your data and settings, and restore the previous device's data and settings even when you do not have it. Refer to Samsung Cloud for further information.

- **Google Drive**: Keep your personal information, app data, and settings safe on your smartphone. You can back up your sensitive information. You must have to sign in to your Google account to back up data.
- **Smart Switch**: Launch Smart Switch and transfer data from your old device. Refer to *Transferring data from your previous device (Smart Switch)* for additional information.

NOTE: Back up your data often to a safe location, such as Samsung Cloud or a computer, so that you can restore it if the data is corrupted or lost due to an accidental factory data reset.

Samsung Cloud

Back up your smartphone's data to Samsung Cloud and restore it later.

Backing up data

You can back up your smartphone's data to Samsung Cloud.

1 From the Settings screen, click **Accounts and backup** and click **Back up data** under **Samsung Cloud**.
2 Mark items you want to back up and click **Back up**.
3 Click **Done**.

NOTE:

- All of your data will not be backed up. To check which data will be backed up, on the Settings screen, click **Accounts and backup** and click **Back up data** under **Samsung Cloud**.

- To check the backup data for other devices in your Samsung Cloud, Go to the Settings screen, click **Accounts and backup** → **Restore data** → ▼, and then choose a device you want.

Restoring data

You can restore your backup data from Samsung Cloud to your smartphone.

1 From the Settings screen, click **Accounts and backup**.

2 Click **Restore data** → ▼ and choose a device you want.

3 Mark items you want to restore and click **Restore**.

CHAPTER NINE:

ADVANCED SETTINGS

Advanced features

Options

Activate advanced features and modify the settings that control each feature.

From the Settings screen, click **Advanced features**.

- **Call & text on other devices**: Use your device's calling and messaging features on other devices that are signed in to your Samsung account.

- **Continue apps on other devices**: Use your device's apps on other devices that are signed in to your Samsung account.

- **Link to Windows**: Promptly access data saved in your device on your computer. Refer to *Link to Windows* for further details.

- **Android Auto**: Connect your device to a vehicle and control some of your device's features on the vehicle's display.

- **Side key**: Select an app or feature to start using the Side key. Refer to *Setting the Side key* for further information.

- **Motions and gestures**: Activate the motion feature and organize settings. Refer to *Motions and gestures* for additional information.

- **One-handed mode**: Activate one-handed operation mode for your convenience when using the smartphone with one hand.

- **Bixby Routines**: Add routines to automate settings that you use frequently. Your smartphone also recommends useful routines according to your frequent activities. Refer to *Bixby Routines* for additional information.

- **Screenshots and screen recorder**: Modify the settings for screenshots and screen recorder.

- **Show contacts when sharing content**: Make the device to display the people you contacted on the sharing options panel to let you share content directly.

- **Game Launcher**: Activate the Game Launcher. Refer to *Game Launcher* for additional information.

- **Dual Messenger**: Install the second app. Use two distinct accounts for the same messenger app. Refer to *Dual Messenger* for more details.

NOTE: Some features may be unavailable depending on the service provider or model.

Motions and gestures

Activate the motion feature and configure settings.

From the Settings screen, click **Advanced features** → **Motions and gestures**.

- **Lift to wake**: Make the device to turn on the screen anytime you pick it up.

- **Double tap to turn on screen**: Make the device to turn on the screen by double-tapping anywhere on the screen while it's is turned off.

- **Double tap to turn off screen**: Make the device to turn off the screen when you double-tap an empty area on the Home screen or the locked screen.

- **Keep screen on while viewing**: Make the device to stop the display from turning off while you are looking at it.

- **Alert when phone picked up**: Make the device to prompt you if you have missed calls or new messages whenever you pick up the device.

  NOTE: This feature may not respond if the device's screen is turned on or the device is not placed on a flat surface.

- **Mute with gestures**: Make the device to mute some kind of sounds by using motions or gestures.

- **Palm swipe to capture**: Make the device to capture a screenshot when you swipe your hand to the left or right across the screen. You can view the captured images in your device's **Gallery**. Some apps and features will not allow you to capture a screenshot while using them.

NOTE: Excessive shaking or an impact to the device may cause an input that is not intended in situations of some features using sensors.

Video call effects

During video calls, you may use several options such as altering the background.

Press Advanced features, then Video call effects while on the Settings screen, then tap the switch to turn it on. The 🔘 icon will be placed to the screen of the video calling app.

Making use of video call effects

Tap 🔘 on the screen of the video calling app.

• Reset all: Reset all of the settings.

• Background: During video calls, change or blur the background.

• Auto framing: Turn on or off the feature of auto framing. When you enable this function, the device adjusts the filming angle and zoom automatically during video conversations by recognizing and tracking individuals.

• Settings: Choose from a variety of backdrop colors and graphics to use during video conversations.

NOTE:

• Depending on the model, some functionalities may be unavailable.

• Some functionalities are only available when the front camera is used.

Dual Messenger

Install another app and use two distinct accounts for the same messenger app.

1 From the Settings screen, click **Advanced features** → **Dual Messenger**.

   Supported apps will show.

2 Click the switch of an app to install the second app and you will have it installed. The second app's icon will be shown with ⊚.

Second app

NOTE:

- Depending on the app, the Dual Messenger feature may not be available.

- The second app may have limited features.

Uninstalling a second app

1 From the Settings screen, click **Advanced features** → **Dual Messenger**.

2 Click the switch of the app you want to uninstall and click **Uninstall**. Every data relating to the second app will be deleted from the device.

NOTE: If the first app is uninstalled, the second app will also be deleted.

Digital Wellbeing and parental controls

View the history of your device usage and use features to stop your device from meddling with your life. You may also like to set up parental controls for your children and manage their digital use.

From the Settings screen, click **Digital Wellbeing and parental controls**.

- **Screen time**: Set goals for how much you use your device daily.

- **App timers**: Limit each app's daily usage time by setting a timer. When you get to the limit, the app will be deactivated and you will not be able to use it more.

- **Focus mode**: Activate focus mode. This helps you to avoid distractions from your device and stay focused on what you want. You can allow some apps to be used in focus mode.

- **Bedtime mode**: Activate bedtime mode to reduce eye strain before you go to sleep and prevent you from being disturbed while sleeping.

- **Parental controls**: Take charge of your children's digital use.

Battery and device care

Introduction

The device care feature gives you a summary of the position of your device's battery, storage, memory, and system security. You are also able to automatically optimize the device by simply tapping with your finger.

Optimizing your device

From the Settings screen, click **Battery and device care** →
Optimize now.

The quick optimization feature enhances the device performance through the following means:

- Helping to close apps that may be running in the background.
- Managing unusual battery usage.
- Scanning for any crashed apps and malware in your device.

Using the auto optimization feature

Your device can be set to perform auto optimization when it is not in use. Click ⧗ → **Automation** → **Auto optimize daily** and click the switch to activate it. If you want to define the time to perform auto optimization, click **Time**.

Battery

Check the remaining battery power and how long you can use the device. If your devices has low battery level, conserve battery power by activating power saving features.

From the Settings screen, click **Battery and device care** →
Battery.

- **Power saving mode**: Activate power saving mode to lengthen the battery's usage time.

- **Background usage limits**: Limit battery usage for apps that you do not use frequently.

- **More battery settings**: Configure advanced battery settings.

NOTE:

- The usage time left shows how long more you can use the device before the battery power runs out. Usage time left may by device settings and operating conditions.

- You may not receive notifications from some apps when using power saving mode.

Storage

Check the status of the used memory as well as the available memory.

From the Settings screen, click **Battery and device care** → **Storage**. To delete files or uninstall apps that you no longer use, choose a category. Then, click and hold, or choose, an item and click **Delete** or **Uninstall**.

NOTE:

- The actual available capacity of the internal memory is usually less than the stated capacity. This is because the operating system and default apps occupy part of the memory.

  The available capacity may change still anytime you update the device.

- To view the available capacity of the internal memory, access the Specification section for your device on the Samsung website.

Memory

From the Settings screen, click **Battery and device care → Memory**.

To speed up your device by stopping apps running in the background, mark apps from the apps list, and click **Clean now**.

Device protection

Check the security status of your device. This feature helps to scan your device for malware.

From the Settings screen, click **Battery and device care → Device protection → Scan phone**.

Apps

Manage the apps in your device and change their settings. You are able to view the apps' usage information, change their notification or permission settings, or uninstall or disable any unnecessary apps.

From the Settings screen, click **Apps**.

General management

Personalize your device's system settings or reset the device.

From the Settings screen, click **General management**.

- **Language**: Choose device languages. Refer to *Adding device languages* for more details.

- **Text-to-speech output**: Change the settings for text-to-speech features to make use of when you activate TalkBack. For instance, you can modify languages, speed, and more.

- **Date and time**: Access and modify the settings to control how your device displays the time and date.

NOTE: If the battery becomes completely discharged, the time and date is reset.

- **Samsung Keyboard settings**: Alter the settings for the Samsung keyboard.

- **Keyboard list and default**: Choose a keyboard to use by default and alter the keyboard settings.

- **Physical keyboard**: Alter the settings for an external keyboard.

- **Mouse and trackpad**: Alter the settings for an external mouse or trackpad.

- **Autofill service**: Choose an autofill service to use.

- **Reset**: Reset the settings of your device or execute a factory data reset.

- **Contact us**: Make an enquiry or view frequently asked questions.

Adding device languages

Add more languages to use on your device.

1 From your Settings screen, click **General management** → **Language** → **Add language**. If you like to view all the languages you can possibly add, click ⋮ → **All languages**.

2 Choose a language to add.

3 To set the chosen language as the default language, click **Set as default**. To retain the current language setting, click **Keep current**.

The chosen language will be added to your languages list. If you have modified the default language, the chosen language will be added to the top of the list.

To alter the default language from your languages list, choose the language you want and click **Apply**. If there's any app that doesn't support the default language, the next supported language in the list will be used instead.

Accessibility

Configure various settings in your device to improve its accessibility.

From the Settings screen, click **Accessibility**.

- **Recommended for you**: Find out about the accessibility features you are currently using and see other recommended features you may like.

- **TalkBack**: Activate TalkBack, which offers you voice feedback. To view help information to know more about how you can use this feature, click **Settings** → **TalkBack tutorial**.

- **Visibility enhancements**: Personalize the settings to improve accessibility for users with impaired vision.

- **Hearing enhancements**: Personalize the settings to enhance accessibility for users with hearing impairment.

- **Interaction and dexterity**: Personalize the settings to enhance accessibility for users who have low dexterity.

- **Advanced settings**: Configure settings concerning Direct access and notification features.

- **Installed services**: View accessibility services installed on your smartphone.

- **About Accessibility**: Take a look at the Accessibility information.

- **Contact us**: Make enquiry or view frequently asked questions.

Software update

Update the software of your smartphone through the firmware over-the-air (FOTA) service. You can also plan software updates.

From the Settings screen, click **Software update**.

- **Download and install**: Find out about updates and install them manually.

- **Auto download over Wi-Fi**: Make the device to download updates automatically whenever it's connected to a Wi-Fi network.

- **Last update**: Review information about the last software update.

NOTE: Whenever there are emergency software updates which are meant to secure your device and to block new types of security threats, they will be installed automatically without your consent.

Security updates information

Security updates are meant to strengthen the security of your device and protect your personal information from external threats. For security updates for your device's model, visit *security.samsungmobile.com*.

NOTE: The website does not support all languages.

About phone

Access useful information about your device.

From the Settings screen, click **About phone**.

To modify your device's name, click **Edit**.

- **Status information**: Take a look at a number of device information, such as the SIM card status, Wi-Fi MAC address, and serial number.
- **Legal information**: Access legal information concerning the device, such as safety information and the open source license.

- **Software information**: See the software information of your smartphone, such as the versions of its operating system and firmware.

- **Battery information**: Show the device's battery status and information.

CHAPTER TEN:

CARE AND MAINTENANCE

Precautions for using the device

Please take time to read this manual before using the device to guarantee safe and proper use.

- The descriptions used here are based on the device's default settings.

- Some of the content in your device may not be the same depending on your region or service provider. It may also vary by model specifications, or device's software.

- The device may need a connection to a Wi-Fi or mobile network when you are using some apps or features.

- Content (high quality content) that needs high CPU and RAM usage will inevitably affect the general performance of the device. Apps associated to the content may not work correctly depending on the device's specifications and the environment that it is used in.

- Samsung does not take legal responsibility for any performance problems that may be caused by apps gotten from other sources than Samsung.

- Samsung does not take legal responsibility for any performance problems or incompatibilities arising from edited registry settings or modified operating system software. Trying to customize the operating system may cause the device or apps to work inappropriately.

- Software, sound sources, wallpapers, images, and other media supplied with this device are licensed for restricted use. Extracting and using these materials for commercial or other purposes is a violation of copyright laws. Users are fully accountable for illegal use of media.

- You may have to pay extra charges for data services, such as messaging, uploading and downloading, auto-syncing, or using location services which are dependent on your existing data plan. For large data transfers, it is advisable to use the Wi-Fi feature.

- Default apps that come along with the device are liable to updates and may no longer be supported without previous notice. If you have queries about an app provided with the device, you can contact a Samsung Service Centre. For user-installed apps, contact your service providers.

- Modifying the device's operating system or installing software from unauthorized sources may cause the device to malfunction, result in data corruption or loss. These actions equate to violations of your Samsung license agreement and will render your warranty void.

- Depending on the region you live or your service provider, a screen protector is usually attached to your device for protection during production and distribution. Although, your warranty does not cover any damage to the screen protector.

- You'll be able see the touchscreen clearly even in strong outdoor sunlight by automatically adjusting the contrast range depending on the surrounding environment. Owing to the nature of the device, displaying fixed graphics for extended periods may cause afterimages (screen burn-in) or ghosting.

  − It is advisable not to use fixed graphics on part or all of the touchscreen for a long period and turn off the touchscreen when the device is not in use.

  − You can set the touchscreen to turn off automatically when it is not in using. From the **Settings** app, tap **Display** → **Screen timeout**, and then choose the length of time you want the device to wait before turning off the touchscreen.

- – If you want to set the touchscreen to automatically adjust its brightness based on the immediate environment, launch the **Settings** app, tap **Display**, and then tap the **Adaptive brightness** switch to activate it.

- Depending on the region or model, some devices may need authorization from the Federal Communications Commission (FCC).

  If your device is permitted by the FCC, you can view the FCC ID of the device. To see the FCC ID, go to the **Settings** app and launch, then tap **About phone → Status information**. If your device does not have an FCC ID, it means that the device has not been approved for sale in the U.S. or its territories. In that case, it may only be brought to the U.S. for the owner's personal use.

- The use of mobile devices on aeroplanes or ships depend on applicable federal and local guidelines and restrictions. Find out from appropriate authorities and always follow crew instructions about when and how you may use your device.

- You can view the regulatory information on the device depending on your region. To see the information, open the **Settings** app and click **About phone** → **Regulatory information**.

- Please note that your device has magnets. You are therefore advised to keep it safely from objects that may have any interference with magnets such as credit cards and implantable medical devices. If you have an implantable medical device, you're advised to consult your physician before using this device.

Maintaining water and dust resistance

Your device is water- and dust-resistant. Ensure you follow these tips cautiously to preserve the water- and dust-resistance of your device. Failure to do so may lead to damage of your device.

- Do not dip the device in fresh water deeper than 1 m or keep it submerged for more than 30 minutes. If you plunge the device in any liquid other than fresh water, such as salt water, ionised water, or alcoholic beverage, liquid will enter the device faster.

- Avoid exposing the device to **water moving with force**.

- If the device is exposed to fresh water, dry it carefully with a clean, soft cloth. If the device is exposed to other liquids, such as salt water, swimming pool water, soapy water, oil, perfume, sunscreen, hand cleaner, or chemical products such as cosmetics, rinse it with fresh water and dry it painstakingly with a clean, soft cloth. Failure to follow these instructions may affect the device's performance and appearance.

- **If the device has been submerged in water or the microphone or speaker is wet,** you may have problems hearing sound clearly during a call. After wiping the device with a dry cloth, dry it painstakingly before using it.

- The device's touchscreen plus other features may malfunction **if the device is used in water**.

- **A severe fall of a hard impact on the device** may damage the water- and dust-resistant features of the device.

- Your smartphone has been duly tested in a controlled environment and under specific conditions, and consequently certified to be water- and dust-resistant. (It has satisfied the requirements of classification IP67 as defined by the international standard IEC 60529-Degrees of Protection provided by Enclosures [IP Code]; test conditions: 15-35 °C, 86-106 kPa, fresh water, 1 metre, 30 minutes). Notwithstanding this classification, there is yet the possible for your device to be damaged in certain conditions.

Instructional icons

Warning: circumstances that could cause injury to yourself or others

Caution: circumstances that could cause damage to your device or other equipment

Note: notes, usage tips, or additional information

Device overheating situations and solutions

When the device overheats during the process of charging the battery

In the process of charging, the device and its charger may become hot. It may even feel hotter to the touch during wireless charging or fast charging. This is normal and does not affect the device's lifespan or performance. If the battery becomes excessively hot, the charging speed may decrease or the charger may stop charging.

Do the following when the device heats up:

- Remove the device from the charger and close any running apps. Wait for the device to cool down and then resume charging the device again.

- If the lower part of the device overheats, it may be that the USB cable connected is damaged. Simply replace the damaged USB cable with a new Samsung-approved one.

- If you use a wireless charger for your device, never place foreign objects, such as metallic objects, magnets, and magnetic stripe cards, amid the device and the wireless charger.

NOTE: The wireless charging or fast charging feature is limited to only supported models.

When the device heats up during use

When using features or apps that utilize more power or use them for extended periods, your device may temporarily heat up because of increased battery consumption. Close any running apps and allow the device to cool down for a while.

The following are examples of circumstances in which the device may overheat. Since your device's functions and apps may vary, the examples below may not apply to your model.

- During the initial setup after purchase or when restoring data • When downloading large files
- When using apps that require more power or using apps for prolonged periods:
  - When playing high-quality games for prolonged periods
  - When recording videos for prolonged periods
  - When streaming videos with the device set to the maximum brightness setting
  - When connecting to a TV
- When the device is doing multiple tasks concurrently (or, when running many apps in the background):
  - When using Multi window.
  - When you're updating or installing apps and recording videos at the same time.
  - When you're downloading large files while making a video call

- When recording videos and at the same time, using a navigation app

- When you're making use of large amount of data for syncing your accounts with, for instance, the cloud or email.

- When using a navigation app in a car and you place the device in direct sunlight

- When the device's mobile hotspot and tethering feature is in use

- When the device being used in areas where there is weak signals or poor reception.

- When the device's battery is being charged with a damaged USB cable

- When the smartphone's multipurpose jack is damaged or unprotected against foreign materials, such as liquid, dust, metal powder, and pencil lead

- When you're roaming

Do the following when the device heats up:

- Always keep the device updated with the latest software.

- If there's conflicts between running apps, it may cause the device to heat up. Restart the device.

- Deactivate the Wi-Fi, GPS, and Bluetooth features when they are not in use.

- Close apps that increase battery consumption or that run in the background whenever they're not in use.

- Delete unnecessary files or unused apps.

- Decrease the brightness of the screen.

- If the device overheats or feels hot for an extended period, do not use it for a while. If the overheating persists, contact a Samsung Service Centre.

Precautions for device overheating

If you begin to feel uncomfortable as a result of the device overheating, stop using the device.

When the device heats up, limited features and performance may ensue or the device may turn off to cool down. The feature is only available on supported models.

- If the device overheats and reaches a certain temperature, you'll receive a warning message to prevent device failure, skin irritations and damages, and battery leakage. To bring down the temperature of the device, the screen brightness will be reduced, the performance speed will be limited and battery charging will stop. Also, any running apps will be closed and all calling and other features will be limited, except for emergency calls, till when the device cools down.

- If you receive the second message due to a further increase of the device's temperature, the device will turn off automatically. Allow the device's temperature to cool down below the specified level before using the device. If you receive the second warning message during an emergency call, the call will not be disconnected by a forced shut down.

Precautions for operating environment

Your device may heat up as a result of extreme weather conditions in the surrounding environment. Beware of the following conditions and take care to avoid shortening the battery's lifespan, damaging the device, or causing a fire:

- Do not keep your device in very cold or very hot temperatures.

- Do not expose your device to direct sunlight for prolonged periods.

- Do not use or keep your device for prolonged periods in very hot areas, such as inside a car during the summertime.

- Avoid placing the device in any areas that may overheat, such as on an electric heating mat.

- Never keep your device near or in heaters, microwaves, hot cooking equipment, or high-pressure containers.

- Do not use a naked or damaged cable, and do not use any charger or battery that is either damaged or malfunctioning.

CHAPTER ELEVEN:
TROUBLESHOOTING TIPS

Before you eventually contact a Samsung Service Centre, please try the following solutions, although some conditions may not apply to your device.

You may also find Samsung Members handy to solve any problems you might experience while using your device.

When your device prompts you to enter one of the following codes while using it or when you turn on the device:

- Password: If you have enabled the device lock feature, you must enter the password you set for the device.

- PIN: When you want to use your smartphone for the first time or when you enable the PIN requirement, you must enter the PIN supplied with the SIM or USIM card. However, you can disable the feature by simply using the Lock SIM card menu.

- PUK: This means your SIM or USIM card has been blocked, usually because you have entered your PIN incorrectly several times. You must enter the PUK supplied with SIM or USIM card by your service provider.

- PIN2: When you access a menu that needs the PIN2, you must enter the PIN2 supplied with the SIM or USIM card. For more information about this issue, contact your service provider.

If your device is showing network or service error messages

- This usually happens as a result of weak signals or poor reception, making your device to lose reception. Try move away from your current area to another area. While moving, error messages may show again severally.

- You need a subscription to access some options in your device or its apps. For further information, contact your service provider.

Your device refuses to turn on

When the battery is utterly discharged, your device will not turn on. Charge the battery fully before turning on the device.

The touchscreen does not respond properly or is responding slowly.

- This may be as a result of a screen protector or other optional accessories attached to the touchscreen.

- If you're putting on hand gloves, if your hands are not clean while touching the touchscreen, or if you're tapping the screen with your fingertips or with sharp objects, the touchscreen may not function properly.
- The touchscreen may not function well in humid conditions or when it is exposed to water. So ensure the touchscreen is clean and dry.
- Restart your device to be sure it's cleared of any temporary software bugs.
- Confirm that your device software is updated to the latest version.
- If you have your device's touchscreen scratched or damaged, visit a Samsung Service Centre.

Your device freezes or experiences a fatal error

Experiment the following solutions. If the problem persists, contact a Samsung Service Centre.

Restarting the device

If your device is freezing or hanging intermittently, you may need to close all open apps or turn off the device and turn it on again.

Forcing restart

If your device is frozen and unresponsive, press and hold the Side key and the Volume Down key together at the same time for more than 7 seconds to restart it.

Resetting the device

If the methods above do not solve your problem, do a factory data reset.

Start the **Settings** app and click **General management** → **Reset** → **Factory data reset** → **Reset** → **Delete all**. Before performing the factory data reset, make sure you have a backup copy of important data stored in your device.

Calls are not connected

- Confirm that you have accessed the right cellular network.
- Check if you have set call barring for the phone number you are dialing. If you have done so, your call will not connect.
- Confirm that you have not set call barring for the incoming phone number.

Others cannot hear you when making a call

- Make sure that you do not cover the built-in microphone by any means.

- Make sure that you place the microphone close to your mouth.
- If you're using an earphone, make sure that it is properly connected.

You hear sound echoes during a call

Regulate the volume by pressing the Volume key or move to another area.

A cellular network or the Internet is frequently disconnected or poor audio quality

- Make sure that you're not blocking the device's internal antenna.
- When you are in areas where there are weak signals or poor reception, you may lose reception. Problems of connectivity may be associated with the service provider's base station. Change your location and try again.
- When you are using the device while moving, wireless network services may be disabled as a result of problems with the service provider's network.

The battery doesn't charge well (For Samsung-approved chargers)

- Make sure the charger is connected properly.
- Visit a Samsung Service Centre for a replacement of the battery.

The battery depletes faster than when you first purchased it

- Exposure of the device or the battery to very cold or very hot temperatures, may reduce the useful charge.
- Consider the apps and other features you use. Battery consumption increases with certain features or apps, such as GPS, games, or the Internet.
- The battery is expendable and the useful charge reduces over time. Consider replacing your expended battery.

Error messages pop up when launching the camera

You must have enough available memory and battery power to operate the camera app. If you get error messages when starting the camera, try the following:

- Charge the battery.
- Free up some space in your memory by transferring files to a computer or deleting files from your device.
- Restart the device. If the problem still persists with the camera app after trying these tips, contact a Samsung Service Centre.

Picture quality is poorer than the preview

- The quality of your pictures depends on the surroundings and the photography techniques you apply.

- Taking pictures in dark areas, at night, or indoors may cause image noise or make images to be captured out of focus.

Error messages pop up when opening multimedia files

If you receive error messages or you're unable to play multimedia files on your device, try the following:

- Free up some space in your device memory by transferring files to a computer or deleting files from your device.

- Check if the music file is Digital Rights Management (DRM)-protected. If it is, you must provide the appropriate license or key to play the file.

- Make sure that the file formats are supported by your device. If the file format is not supported, such as DivX or AC3, install the relevant app that supports it. To check the file formats that your device supports, visit the Samsung website.

- Your device supports pictures and videos that are captured with it. Pictures and videos captured by other devices may not be supported.

- Your device supports multimedia files that are authenticated by your network service provider or providers of additional services. You may have problems working with some content from the Internet, such as ringtones, videos, or wallpapers.

Bluetooth is not working well

Another Bluetooth device may be located or there may be connection problems or performance malfunctions. Otherwise, try the following:

- Make sure the device you want to connect with is ready to be scanned or connected to.
- Make sure that your device and the other Bluetooth device are within the maximum Bluetooth range which is 10m.
- On your device, start the **Settings** app, click **Connections**, and then click the **Bluetooth** switch to activate again.
- On your device, start the **Settings** app, click **General management** → **Reset** → **Reset network settings** → **Reset settings** → **Reset** to reset network settings. Your registered information may be lost when performing the reset.

If the above tips do not resolve the problem, contact a Samsung Service Centre.

The screen brightness adjustment bar does not show on the notification panel

Open the notification panel by pulling the status bar downwards, and then pull the notification panel downwards. Click ↕ → **Quick panel layout** and click the **Show brightness control above notifications** switch to activate it.

Unable to established a connection when you connect the device to a computer

- Make sure you are using a compatible USB cable with your device.
- Make sure you have the proper driver installed on your computer and that it's up-to-date.

Your device cannot find your current location

GPS signals may be obstructed by buildings or other conditions in some locations. In such circumstances, set the device to use Wi-Fi or a mobile network to find your current location.

Data stored in the device has been lost

Always have a backup copy of every important data stored in the device. Otherwise, you cannot bring back your data if it is corrupted or lost. Samsung will not be held accountable for the loss of data stored in the device.

A small gap shows around the outside of the device case

- This gap is an essential manufacturing feature and some slight rocking or vibration of parts may take place.

- With the lapse of time, friction between parts may lead to slight expansion of this gap.

There is insufficient space in the device's storage

Delete any redundant data, such as cache, by making use of the device care feature or you can manually delete fallow apps or files to free up storage space.

The Home button does not appear

The navigation bar which contains the Home button may disappear when using some apps or features. To view the navigation bar, pull upwards from the bottom of the screen.

Removing the battery

- **If you want to remove the battery for any reason, contact an authorized service centre. To get instructions on how to remove battery, please visit www.samsung.com/global/ecodesign_energy.**

- For your safety, you **must not try to remove** the battery by yourself. If the battery is not properly removed, it may result in damage to the battery and/or device, cause personal injury, and/or result in the device being unsafe to use.

- Samsung does not accept any legal responsibility for any damage or loss (whether in contract or tort, including negligence) which may ensue from failure to exactly follow these warnings and instructions, save for death or personal injury caused by Samsung's negligence.

INDEX

INCREASE RING TIME —

61101xxx ? #
PRESS CALL BUTTON

Printed in Great Britain
by Amazon

18759983R00139